WHOLE LANGUAGE:
INQUIRING VOICES

Dorothy Watson, Carolyn Burke and Jerome Harste

SCHOLASTIC

Scholastic Canada Ltd.
123 Newkirk Road, Richmond Hill, Ontario, Canada L4C 3G5

Scholastic Inc.
730 Broadway, New York, NY 10003, USA

Ashton Scholastic Limited
Private Bag 1, Penrose, Auckland , New Zealand

Ashton Scholastic Pty Limited
PO Box 579, Gosford, NSW, 2250, Australia

Scholastic Publications Ltd.
Holly Walk, Leamington Spa, Warwickshire CV32 4LS, England

Cover photo © Masterfile/Daily Telegraph

7 6 5 4 3 2   Printed in USA   0 1 2 3 4 5/9

Canadian Cataloguing in Publication Data

Watson, Dorothy J. (Dorothy Jo), 1930-
   Whole language: inquiring voices

(Bright Idea)
ISBN 0-590-73371-0

1. Reading (Elementary) - Language Experience
approach. I. Burke, Carolyn L. II. Harste, Jerome C.
III. Title.

LB1573.33.W37 1989   372.4'14   C89-093646-3

Contents

This book is lovingly dedicated to two people,
one quiet and one always on the move:

First to Marie Harper, who laughed at our jokes, heard only our acceptable
language and wondered if all teachers behave the way we do.

Second to our editor, Adrian Peetoom, who heard our voices, encouraged
our inquiry, supported our research and made us better learners.

Nor will we easily forget the kindnesses of the Fike family — Colene,
Richard, David and Kevin — who fed us, read us stories and chased
raccoons from under our feet as we were writing.
To them, our sincere thanks.

Preface

"Hello, Harste, it's Adrian Peetoom again. I'm calling because I still want a Bright Idea book from you."

"I know, but I'm not ready to write it yet. I don't have a topic."

"Nonsense. Write about what you've been thinking about. What have you been speaking on?"

"Teaching as inquiry."

"Well, there you go."

"But I don't believe in writing things alone. I think it's important to make a professional statement that all knowledge is social and collaborative."

"Well then, write it with someone else. Who do you want to write it with?"

"Carolyn Burke and Dorothy Watson. I've written a lot with Carolyn and I'd really like to do something with Dorothy. Last week I presented at the Mark Twain Literacy Conference. Dorothy helped me on a session and I loved what she did."

"That's fine with me. When can we do it?"

"What do you mean?"

"I'll come down for four days and work with you. You exchange ideas and I'll help you write them up."

"You're kidding me. A book in four days! Man, you don't understand how I write."

"Yes, I do. Slow. And we're going to fix that."

"Good luck. And if you think I'm bad, you haven't seen Watson and Burke!"

"Tell me about teaching as inquiry."

"Well, as you know I've been a strong supporter of the notion of using children as informants. Essentially I want teachers to understand inquiry as a way of understanding children in classrooms, and the teaching-learning relationship as one in which children act as informants. I also think that perceiving teaching as inquiry is the direction whole language has to take.

"When I was at a conference this summer a teacher said to me she was 'doing Graves.' That scares me. It means teachers are seeing whole language as an orthodoxy rather than a vehicle for self-renewal and learning. I think there's some real urgency to change these perceptions if we don't want whole language to stagnate."

"Is that what you and Dorothy did your session on at the Mark Twain Conference?"

"Yes."

"Tell me what you did."

"We began by arguing that recent advancements in sociology, psychology and linguistics created whole language and that what whole language essentially does is challenge traditional notions about teaching. We went through such things as curriculum, scope and sequence, and instructional grouping, evaluation, focus and relevance, showing how new information is upsetting old 'truths.' And we talked about the kind of research whole language people are doing in each of these areas. We tried to demonstrate that whole language is also changing, and invited teachers to be part of the movement. We wanted to get across the notion that whole language isn't an orthodoxy — there's no one right way to do it — but rather that it's an invitation to inquiry, an invitation for teachers to take charge of their classroom once again."

"Specifics, please."

"Okay. Relative to scope and sequence, for example, we said that whole language researchers have shown there's no inherent order in the way language is learned. This finding has undermined the whole notion of skills instruction. The new question is, 'But if I can't use skills as a device for organizing curriculum, what can I use?'

"We then showed how some people are using the cycle that writers go through as a way of organizing their curriculum. At the end of our discussion of each curricular area we invited the teachers to form small groups to explore other metaphors they might use for organizing their own curricula, and recommended that they pick one of the ideas for a research project."

"That sounds great. Tell me about the other curricular areas you covered."

"Well, let's take instructional grouping. We argued that language researchers are finding that we learned most of what we know from being in the presence of others, not from direct instruction. We talked about the curricular implications of this idea and the reasons for so much emphasis now being placed on collaboration.

"For instructional approach, we talked about our feeling that in the final analysis our interest in reading and writing is an interest in learning. We then discussed the curricular implications of this conclusion and the kinds of research being done by whole language teachers, and invited them to think about the implications for their own classrooms.

"We followed the same format for assessment (the goal of evaluation is self-evaluation), instructional strategies (learning is defined as a search for patterns that connect), instructional match (culture isn't something that can be left on the steps of the school) and instructional relevance (if you haven't seen a real language user do it outside of school, throw it out).

"With these ideas on the floor we talked about how and why whole language researchers are exploring such diverse topics as language-rich environments, open-ended classroom activities, invitations, literature-based reading programs, collaboration, reflexivity, negotiated curriculum, alternate communication systems, empowerment, the politics of literacy and the relationship between literacy and citizenship. We stressed that the data isn't in yet, that whole language will be enriched by hearing new voices: their voices."

"Wow, that should make a great book. Call me when the three of you have four days free."

Listening to different drummers

Three teachers

Laura has no doubt about teaching and learning. She works very hard at teaching and her students work very hard at learning. The school district provides her with a detailed outline of her curriculum. Periodic standardized tests and end-of-level basal reader exams measure the children's learning. Because parents and their opinions are important to Laura, she sends reports home every eight weeks.

Leonard places students at the center of his curriculum, paying careful attention to their needs and interests. He takes the best of the official mandates and puts them together with the concerns and interests of his students to shape the curriculum. He's an experienced kid-watcher who constantly monitors the children's growth and invites them to take stock of their own learning. For reporting to parents Leonard uses long notes, telephone calls and conferences.

Marne focuses on issues generated by herself and her students. Her expectations and her students' persistent and compelling questions are the propelling forces of their curriculum. Together she and they take responsibility for the evaluation of their personal and social learning, as well as for the advancement of their curricular experiences. Parents, teacher and students promote the natural force of inquiry in partnership, through direct involvement in a variety of learning endeavors.

Laura, Leonard and Marne: three excellent and successful teachers liked by their students and respected by their colleagues. Yet they are very different from each other. How do we account for these differences, and for the fact that their classrooms are quite diverse in tone, atmosphere and curriculum? We invite you to study them as educators and, in doing so, to investigate yourself as a teacher as well.

As you read this chapter you will begin to experience the pattern of the book. By making it possible for you to observe and ask questions about children and other teachers as learners, we hope to help you become more thoughtful about yourself as a learner so that, gradually, you find yourself concentrating on your own learning as well as theirs. This first chapter sets the stage.

Reflections

A good way to get to know people is to listen to the questions they ask. When we find out what a person is curious about, we get glimpses of the motivating forces that determine the focus of that person's time, energy and efforts. With teachers, we begin to understand what they value and what rationale underlies their practices.

So what types of questions do Laura, Leonard and Marne (and you) ask? Where and when does their (and your) inquiry take place and which people do they (and you) choose to question? Let's look at their various inquiries into teaching and learning, curriculum, evaluation and parental influence.

Laura

Laura's most urgent questions have to do with evaluation. She's eager to learn what her students are expected to know, what they are accountable for on mandated tests. Information concerning the content and procedures of the tests lead to one major inquiry: How can my curriculum best be arranged to ensure that my students have mastered the necessary information and will therefore score well on the exams?

When Laura's students don't meet her or their parents' expectations, or those of the district administrators, she turns to teachers' manuals and the district's prescribed curriculum. She works even harder within the confines of her lesson plans and concentrates on the discrete skills she feels will add up to mastery of the subject for her students. She searches for units and activities that fit into the prescribed curriculum and carefully follows the steps suggested.

Laura encourages the students to ask questions; she wants them to understand what her goals and objectives are for their study. She makes herself available to parents as well and conscientiously reports test scores and classroom behavior. She's curious about family literacy experiences but finds it difficult to frame suitable questions; it seems more appropriate for her to inform the parents than to be informed by them.

Leonard

Leonard's important questions differ from Laura's. While keeping the curriculum clearly in mind, he focuses on student roles. He studies his learners and asks questions about them, probing not only their needs and interests but also the ways they perceive their own learning. Answers to his questions help him orchestrate and facilitate their efforts and energies and set curriculum in motion.

When Leonard needs help, he asks questions about the growth patterns and development of children in his class's age group. He bases his questions on what he sees as both strengths and weaknesses in his particular students. He talks with members of his teacher support group (Teachers Applying Whole Language — TAWL) and regularly takes their advice or modifies one of their teaching strategies for his own use.

He invites students to ask questions and uses those questions to help them understand what they know about science, math and social studies. They also know the value of questioning in their literature study.

Leonard consults with parents as partners and provides, as well as receives, information that will promote learning. Parents feel comfortable visiting his classroom and regularly assist in classroom projects.

Marne

For Marne inquiry is a way of life. She constantly asks questions of herself, her students and their parents. She questions potential content of the curriculum (what will we think about?) and conditions of teaching and learning (how will we do it?). She feels that both teaching and learning are dimensions of inquiry and believes that every individual must have the opportunity to be both teacher and student. Each member of her classroom, including herself, is considered a learner, as are others outside the classroom who are interested in the children — parents, for instance.

Marne invites investigation by ensuring a comfortable setting for all learners: students, teacher and parents. Within the safe haven of the classroom it becomes possible to ask questions that make a difference in the thinking, even the lives, of the learners. She expects answers that will contribute to curriculum and to the learning atmosphere of the classroom.

Every member of this community of learners moves in and around the center of the curriculum, taking on various appropriate roles — sometimes researcher, resource person, listener, support team member, advocate, presenter or expert, but always inquirer. And when things go wrong, Marne does exactly what she does when all is well — she asks questions of herself, of her students, of the members of her TAWL group, of the strategies used, of anything that may affect the learning environment.

She invites students to inquire into their own abilities and research their own advancement. In addition, there's constant evaluation of the existing program. Process evaluation assures a curriculum that's always in process, always flexible, always alive, always true to the learners.

An invitation

We invite you now to describe yourself in the way we've described Laura, Leonard and Marne. What questions do you ask about learning and teaching, about curriculum, evaluation and parental involvement in your classroom? Which of these categories is most important to you and which areas provide the really tough questions? If other categories are more urgent and compelling for you, ask questions related to them.

Area(s)	Questions
Learning	
Teaching	
Curriculum	
Evaluation	
Parental involvement	

Now take another look at Laura, Leonard, Marne and yourself. How extensive and how intensive are the questions each asks? Do some leave learners (students and teacher) at the surface level of the issues? Do some push the learners over the edge of their current information into new knowledge?

Laura seems to be playing safe with her questions, Leonard less so. He's probing into more areas and doesn't always find the answers comfortable. Marne is even more deeply into real inquiry. She's often pushed into the discomfort zone — an area that's familiar to most whole language teachers.

Marne's inquiries

The remainder of this book will argue that inquiry is a powerful tool of the whole language teacher. Chapter three will describe those conditions of inquiry that distinguish it from the simple act of asking questions.

In classrooms where the pattern of learning is inquiry, you see the following:

- Teacher and students accept *vulnerability* and see it as a spur to real learning.
- Teacher and students experience a *sense of community* in their learning.
- Teacher and students insist that their learning be *generative* — that is, that it lead to action.
- Teacher and students demand *democracy*, insisting that all voices be heard.
- Teacher and students recognize that inquiry is *reflexive*; they see themselves and each other as instruments for their own learning.

Marne's inquiry leads to vulnerability

Daily Marne puts her whole language theories to the test. In doing so, she opens herself to criticism and makes it necessary for her students to do the same. Even the curriculum is vulnerable: inevitably some aspect of it will be less than what Marne envisions. She's willing to take that risk because she's a learner and knows she'll gain new knowledge and new confidence from each experience.

Marne asks:
Can students take on a teacher's role? How can I help them in new learning situations? How will they handle their self-generated course of study and how will they behave while doing so? Will I know when they need me as a teacher — to present strategy lessons, for example, that will move them along with their own inquiry? How can students learn to value

self-assessment and see themselves as cooperative rather than competitive members of a classroom community? How can I help parents become more receptive to taking an active role in the classroom?

Marne's inquiry is set within a community of learners

Members of the community make room for, promote and support the efforts of individuals. Nevertheless, Marne gives students opportunities to realize that by coming together they can make each other look, and feel, a head taller. She deeply believes that the seeking of knowledge is personal, but that the community of learners adds tapestry and depth to an individual's attempts. Her inquiry is framed in a way that lets members of the classroom community know it's possible to recognize another's point of view without having to "buy into" it. Even more, it allows members to disagree outright, but to do so in a way that is supportive of all learners.

Marne asks:
How can a community of learners become collaborative in their efforts? How do we move from merely cooperating in order to achieve some stated goal to truly collaborating in the endeavor? How can students enter a collaborative effort with the understanding that they need not all have the same agenda in the back of their heads, that they need not leave the same experience with identical understandings and knowledge, and that although "the goal" might be reached, it might also be changed, or even abandoned?

Marne's inquiry is generative

Marne's inquiry leads to more extensive and intensive knowledge and makes her comfortable with further action. It educates. Her investigations result from an understanding of her students that incorporates their and her past experiences, from what she perceives their needs are here and now, and from a sense of tomorrow. To be generative in her inquiry Marne must have a vision of the future, and the questions she asks must light the way to that future.

Marne asks:
What kinds of questions reflect past knowledge and are immediately applicable? How is my inquiry generative — that is, where might it lead? When these questions are answered, will the information educate me so I'll become a better inquirer and more proficient in my attempts? How can knowledge be expressed through language, art, song, dance, drama and other creative modes?

Marne's inquiry exists within the democratic structure of the classroom

A democratic setting allows the formerly silent and silenced members of the group to raise their voices when they see fit to do so. Marne doesn't act as if she knows what her students are thinking and feeling. Nor do the students presume to speak for her. Of course they share stories, images and metaphors, and when learners are closely knit they can often finish each other's sentences. But there's utter respect for the individual's thoughts, the individual's questions, the individual's vision, the individual's voice — these must come to life in the democratic society of the classroom. Marne doesn't manipulate her students' minds to her way of thinking by asking a series of questions crafted to arrive at a single correct response.

Marne asks:
What is important and valuable to all the members of our community? How can every voice not only be heard, but be heard to inquire? How can the students and I move in and out of roles so each is both leader and follower? How can teaching and learning, teacher and learner merge?

Marne's inquiry is reflexive

To be reflexive means that, as researchers, learners are able to take a step away and then look back on what they've done, on what they're doing and on where their learning might lead. A reflexive stance empowers learners to look around; they focus not only on the topic at hand, but also on the periphery and beyond — on the spin-offs, the connections made and not made. Marne knows that reflexivity demands space and time for breathing and thinking, as part of the curriculum. Students aren't rushed and they're not told where to begin their reflection. Marne brings out her own natural curiosity and that of her students by starting with the intriguing, the compelling, the relevant.

Marne asks:
What is it that moves and motivates learners? How is it possible to think and rethink process, product and potential? How can all forms of logic be considered and used in learners' investigations? How are my ways of viewing and knowing the same as and different from those of the other learners in this community? How can I help students see that reflexivity is at the heart of evaluation?

One final note

It may seem that Marne inquires about roughly the same things as Laura and Leonard do, question for question, but there's a fundamental difference. Unlike the others, Marne enters the teaching-learning community as one contributing member of it, as a researcher, as a learner, but most of all as one who's willing to trust the other members. For her the classroom community is a community of learners: herself, the children, their parents and all periodic or frequent visitors. Both Laura and Leonard see themselves more as having to regulate, even control, the children's learning.

This fundamental difference becomes clear when we consider where, for each teacher, curriculum is generated. For Laura it's clearly outside the classroom, in broad outlines and specific details. For Leonard it's in the classroom to a point, but made to conform to broad demands that come from outside. For Marne it's in the classroom. She trusts that each learner will bring to the learning community genuine concerns and profound knowledge, knowledge that resides in the culture outside the classroom walls, in the lives of the parents and the neighborhood, in the life of the larger community, and in the events that impinge on the consciousness of one or more of the learners. And about all this we want to talk some more in the next chapter.

Delightfully divergent engagements

Classroom moments that lift the spirits and show the participants in pleasing and productive lights are valued by students and teachers. However, these "engagements" (so called because they are particularly engaging and enticing events) are often seen as mere seasonings to add flavor to the meat and potatoes of the curriculum.

In this chapter we describe three such engagements and look at them as opportunities for developing inquiry in both students and teachers. Each narrative contains an easily recognizable and powerful kernel of inquiry. But for those kernels to grow, purposeful cultivation must be undertaken. So we encourage you to examine the three stories for opportunities taken and opportunities missed.

The play's the thing

Every year Lilly reads the *Lord of the Rings* series to her fourth-graders. Lilly loves the books herself and knows that their clever plots, full of adventure and magic, will appeal to the students' imaginations. For about a month she sits back in her rocking chair for 20 minutes every day and reads aloud. Then, when the final discussion of the final book is finished, she suggests that the class might like to write and produce a play based on the stories. Her suggestion is always joyously accepted.

Since a play must condense the text, first on the agenda is a discussion to select which book events the group wants to use in the play. Next they frame a working outline of the play's scenes. Each student chooses a character and writes a rough draft of that character's dialogue for one of the proposed scenes. Then the group reassembles for casting tryouts.

Students aspiring to a role give a reading of their dialogue. To cast major roles the group votes for the aspirant they feel has written the most effective dialogue for that character. All class members will eventually have some role. Those not elected to a lead will perform as supporting characters and narrators.

At this juncture Lilly takes on her role as executive producer/writer, collecting the dialogues for a busy weekend of rewriting. She crafts each character's part by enhancing the text of the chosen dialogue with the best bits written by other students for that part. She then writes in minor character roles and the narrative in which the action will be embedded.

Tired perhaps, but with mission accomplished, she returns to school on Monday morning with a working draft of the play.

For the next two weeks the usual curriculum functions get compressed or suspended to make room for rehearsals. These are times of concentrated and energetic creativity. The actors play out a variety of interpretations of their characters' actions and explore the relationships with other characters. Alternative, sometimes deeper, interpretations emerge from the text and, if necessary, dialogues are changed to reflect them.

The climax of the experience is reached with a series of three performances for the other classes in the school, and usually one for parents too. Then comes the resolution. The theater lights are switched off, the sets are taken down, the actors go home with traces of makeup still visible on their faces. Every year Lilly is overheard to mutter, "I'm not going through this again next year. It's great, but it takes too much time and effort."

A place of inquiry

For about 10 days each November the heart of sophisticated Toronto, largest city in Canada, is filled with the bleating of sheep, the lowing of cows and the oinking of pigs. The Royal Winter Fair is in town, second largest agricultural exhibition in North America.

Each weekday, yellow school buses arrive, one after the other, and morning visitors have to fight the constant crush of youngsters. What is the attraction?

Over the years school "field trips" to special events and places have grown in popularity, and the Coliseum bulges with attractions. One large wing houses two floors of horses, including several members of international equestrian teams. If you've a mind for it you can wander by the stables to see them quietly munching, watched over constantly by careful grooms. The banners say CANADA, UNITED STATES, WEST GERMANY, MEXICO.

Or perhaps you'd rather take your lunch with you to the ring and watch the competitions. Some horses jump small fences, others walk and run in circles — but how can you tell what it takes to win? P.A. announcements report what's happening, and if you watch you'll soon see patterns that will help you decide the winners and losers before official notification is given. But if you really want to know what makes one horse better than another, find someone who knows — you'll always know who they are — and ask, ask, ask.

If horseflesh isn't your game, you might go to another big wing where you'll meet row upon row of cows, sheep, goats, pigs. You'll also find plenty of birds and rabbits, plain sorts and fancy dans of all kinds.

When you've had enough of animals, you can wander away to find flowers and vegetables, tractors and other farm implements, a craft show. And food: meats, cheeses, butter sculptures, fruits and fudge — for Christmas, of course, though it probably won't last till then.

The Fair is a paradise for the senses. It's also a place to reflect on the environment and its problems: perhaps there's a strange new crop disease or a horde of African bees to fear. It has acres of space and plenty of washrooms, a "field" trip where field crops are only a streetcar ride away from the heart of Toronto. That's why all the yellow school buses, all the eager kids, all the watchful teachers and parent chaperones.

Bert's class is one of the lucky ones. And after their visit he has an agenda for the children: they'll spend a week doing a unit on farm animals. They are to choose an animal that interests them and find out as much as they can about it.

The day before they go he has them review a series of questions he's composed to help them gather the facts. Then off the bus they roll, some with papers flapping loose around their fingers, some armed with official looking clipboards. Here are a few of the questions they have ready:

- Why do farmers raise these animals?
- What care must they have?
- What is their life cycle?
- How expensive are they to raise and what profits are there in raising them?
- What is done with the by-products of these animals?

And because Bert likes a joke, this question is there too: How many eggs does a rooster lay during the year?

Bert has divided the class into interest groups, each with a parent chaperone. First they are to find the animal they are studying and gather their information; then they can go in any direction and explore anything else they want to before they meet in one spot for lunch. So from the big flower display in the lobby the groups go their own ways, one first to the cows, another to the horses, a third to the pigs, a fourth to the rabbits and pigeons. The last group sees an announcement about a dog show — and every farm has a dog, hasn't it?

Some students take their time. They aren't worried about answering all the questions on their sheets because they know that others studying the same animal will collect the information they miss. They stand and watch. It's hard to hold back other questions: How much does a Percheron weigh? How much does he eat? How much does he cost? What does he do on the farm? Why is his mane being braided? How do you keep his coat so glossy?

If they're lucky a keeper may take them to the place where the horses are bathed, with real soap and big streams of lukewarm water. Keepers love to talk about what they do and have done, what they've won and achieved, what they know so well and are expert in. To see what learning looks like you have only to watch the eyes of a youngster glued to the lips of a friendly keeper who's showing off a delicate lamb: talk, talk, stroke, stroke, finally taking the hand of the child, quiet, quiet, stroke, stroke.

But there are always a few students who rush. They approach the animals and their keepers with hurried questions, scribble information in the appropriate empty spaces, and go on. They know what this field trip is for, these question-dancers. Fill the empty spaces. Get the facts. On to the next well of answers. Get it done.

Compelling current context

One December morning Eve's students filed quietly into their classroom. They hung up their coats and picked up their journals from the journal basket, but there the usual routine ended. They didn't greet their friends, read the notes on the message board, find the book they hadn't quite finished the day before, arrange the things they'd need later, then settle down to work. Instead they gathered around their teacher to ask heartfelt questions about something that had happened halfway around the world from their safe and comfortable homes.

These second- and third-grade children, full of compassion and worry, began an inquiry that morning that would educate and inform them about the lives, the culture, and even the politics, of human beings from a distant country. They asked question after question, some perhaps superficial, but some so full of depth and perception that the adults in these children's lives were also touched and caught up in the inquiry. The tragedy of the earthquake victims in Soviet Armenia eclipsed whatever curriculum had been scheduled for that day. Both Eve and the children knew that their lives would be changed because of the destruction and despair that had befallen strangers. With the understanding that comes to the truly concerned, they set aside their journal writing, their individual research projects, even their loved literature study, to pursue this compelling inquiry.

The questions came slowly at first. How many people were killed? Did kids and their pets die? Where is Armenia? Does Soviet mean that they are Russians? Are they Communists? What does their flag look like? Do they talk like us? Were any buildings left? What causes an earthquake? Do we live where earthquakes can happen? Will we have an earthquake in Missouri some day? Is an earthquake worse than a volcano eruption or a hurricane? What about the people who are still alive? Who's helping them? How can we help?

Eve and the children tried as best they could to answer each other's questions, but it became obvious that these inquiries deserved more than a moment's conversation. It was Jody who voiced a common need: "We need to find out." Eve reminded the children that they already had other projects going — she felt she had to. But they felt compelled to get at these questions without delay and were willing to take the consequences of putting their scheduled work aside for the moment. Some clearly indicated their eagerness to put themselves on the line. Their questions and concerns already pointed to outcomes of personal commitment and social action.

The work started as theme studies usually do, but this time with an eagerness not always obvious in the past. The class listed on the board all the topics they could think of, and sub-topics were added over the two weeks. They ranged through Soviet politics, the history of Armenia and the ethnic unrest in the Soviet Union, to the nature of earthquakes and other natural disasters. Individually, in pairs or in trios, the children selected from those topics and a list was created, with the researchers' names placed next to their chosen topics. These were duplicated and distributed to the parents, the librarian and any others who might have information about or interest in the topics.

The children's research abilities were set in motion. In addition to maps, encyclopedias and other conventional resources, they read newspaper and magazine articles, watched the evening news with notepad and pencil in hand, and searched for a variety of human resources. More questions emerged, and the children took more notes than ever before in a research effort. At the end of the first week several asked for help to organize what they'd collected. Eve invited them to meet for a strategy lesson in which she and her student research partner shared how they were organizing their information on "groups that have given help to disaster victims."

The children set a schedule and time limits for themselves: all groups would present their findings to each other within two weeks. The researchers chose their own methods of reporting, although most preferred some form of writing or drawing. They also wanted to make oral reports to their friends, and to the adults who had helped them. Maps were made, charts created and an Armenian song taped, with the help of the music teacher. A geologist came to talk to the class about earthquakes; he had everyone's undivided attention, especially when he spoke about the possibility of a natural disaster in the immediate area.

Points of observation

On first analysis there are two things that stand out about these three events. One is that a deep sense of emotion, commitment and involvement on the part of the learners infused them: the children were involved, they were doing. The second is that all three events are out-of-the-ordinary curricular activities. We don't expect engagements like these to fill an ordinary school day.

So here we meet an anomaly. Why should experiences that appear so delightful and so apparently productive be so infrequent? Let's hold this question in mind as we begin to analyze these three engagements.

Asking questions

The play

Lilly reserves the initiating question for herself. Although she clearly has her students' interests in mind, it's she who chooses the books for their shared reading. Other questions begin to emerge as their reading sessions progress, and come into full power as the children begin to write dialogue and move into rehearsals.

The fair

Like Lilly, Bert reserves the initiation of decisions for himself. The children make their decisions within the context of the constraints he has established. This fact offers a potential explanation for why some of the children rush through the experience: they lack commitment because they lack ownership of the ideas. Another potential explanation has a more constructive nature: it's possible that those who appear to rush do so not because they're not interested, but because the experience is one of their first with farm animals. There's only so much they can take in at one time and only so many distinctions they can draw.

The earthquake

An explosive world event impinges on the personal lives of these learners, offering an invitation for involvement. The children might respond in several ways: ignore it, coolly and passively observe it, or commit themselves to it and invest in it through personal inquiry. They opt for ownership and involvement. No question is too personal, too insignificant, too potentially unanswerable to be raised. The individual learners are not committed to the questions, but to the quest.

For consideration

Freedom requires personal questions.

Freedom as a learner starts with the understanding that each of us must ask our own questions. Who we want to be, what we want to know and where we want to go are all mental purposes over which we maintain control through the generation of personal questions. The questions of others are useful only in the context of our own efforts.

Questions produce more questions.

It's encouraging to understand the service our questions perform as they orient us in our world and set us in motion. Each question we ask provides a new perspective on a familiar landscape, and each new perspective is likely to produce new questions. It's unlikely the questions that serve to initiate our investigation will still be in service at its conclusion.

Conventions inhibit questions.

Some conventional assumptions that continue to operate in education inhibit us from freely and comfortably asking our own questions. The traditional model, which defines the function of education as the transmission of cultural literacy, stresses the value of information and almost totally depends on external learner motivation.

There's been a long tug-of-war between exploration and convention — between invented spelling and standard spelling forms, for instance. When these two forces are kept in balance we have controlled growth and change. But restricting the function of education to that of transmission elevates convention and restricts exploration. The acquisition of conventional knowledge is lauded; asking questions can put that knowledge in danger.

This accounts for the strong and persistent tendency in schools for the students to be supplied with questions as advance organizers. Unfortunately a frequent result is that the students, with no vested interest in the questions, lack self-motivation.

The combined force of these conventional assumptions offers one good explanation for the anomaly we started with. The question then becomes: How long do we relegate stimulating and intuitively useful experiences to an auxiliary role in the school curriculum?

Working with others

The play

A unique feature of this engagement is the number and variety of social relationships the participants engage in. The reading itself is a shared experience, immediately available for interpretation, and it's this perspective each student takes to the apparently individual task of writing dialogue. The rehearsals, which in other contexts would stress consolidating and memorizing, are actually the most liberating and stimulating part of the engagement.

The fair

The questions Bert gives the students for structuring their inquiries are open-ended and will comfortably lead to further related questions, but the students have no part in their formulation. If, instead, the class works together to create a group of questions, then individuals can select the ones they want to use — or compose additional ones for themselves. A truly collaborative research project would allow for a wider breadth of questions, while eliminating redundancy.

The organization of the group also needs to be considered. Students who are interested in the same animal are grouped together and expected to share information. However, it appears that the overriding reason for that arrangement is a monitoring one — Bert's way of assuring adult supervision.

The earthquake

The most important collaborative decision Eve makes is her acknowledgment of the other learners' shared responsibility for formulating curricular decisions. They can debate the possibility of setting aside scheduled projects on the basis of their immediate need to know, as long as they are willing to accept the accompanying responsibilities and consequences.

The public pooling of questions allows people not only to contemplate, but also to contribute thoughts about concerns they personally don't want to pursue. The final set of questions creates a supportive context for the pursuit of individual interests. The ability to work individually or in small groups allows for both shared interests and personal working styles.

For consideration

Is learning private?

The conventional view is that learning is a private, personal and competitive process. Many decisions that favor social educational experiences are inhibited the moment teachers realize it will be difficult, if not impossible, to assign individual responsibility. The evaluation processes which have developed around the "cultural transmission" view of learning have accommodated its purposes by focusing on information transfer and single right answers. Only when we give up this ability to "nail" the individual and no longer worship conventionalized knowledge do we begin to value the social nature of learning and the creative generation of knowledge.

Or is it social?

Learning is best realized in a group when value is placed on each person's uniqueness, when individuals contribute who and what they are, without censure. Diversity ensures increased experience and perspective by setting up anomalies that are resolved by the application of consensus procedures. In this way the group potential becomes available to each individual, a potential far more extensive and varied than any one person can hope to possess. And that potential is available without the need to surrender any dimension of individual personality or perspective.

Where does responsibility lie?

Being wrong a certain percentage of the time is as sure as death and taxes. If this were not the case, inquiry would have no significant place in our lives. We actually use our miscues to monitor our position and our predictions. However, in this imperfect world we are all still responsible for the rules, even for ones we may not (yet) know — much as drivers are held responsible for the rules of the road. Collaboration increases our ability to be reflective about our actions and beliefs, and increases the number of potential solutions we generate.

Creating curriculum

The play

When we consider the play with curriculum in mind, both the obvious flaw and the kernel of inquiry are revealed. This engagement possesses a powerful and completely self-contained life: experiences evolve and develop with each one acting as catalyst for the next. But it has only a tenuous relationship with the ongoing curriculum, a single thread provided by the shared reading component. The oral sharing of books is already a staple of this classroom, but in no other instance does Lilly use it as an invitation to the exploration of undeveloped potentials.

The fair

The fair in the fall, the zoo in the spring. Such repetitive patterns always sacrifice spontaneous curriculum for organizational convenience. Under these conditions, engagements that hold many exciting and mind-stretching potentials become merely colorful but one-dimensional adjuncts to the curriculum — and exciting questions only mask the problem. The educational cart has got itself before the horse. It should be the naturally arising questions that create a demand for the experience.

The earthquake

The curriculum in this classroom is well designed to absorb unexpected events. Because theme units form the major organizing device, the focus is always on issues and the questions that revolve around them. The basic organization remains in place and offers the same support for the unexpected inquiry as it does for the planned.

For consideration

Conventional learning has a price.

There's always a trade-off between economy of thought and action on the one hand and creativity on the other. When we become too concerned with looking over our shoulder we tend to stress conservation, and curriculum becomes a series of preplanned exercises designed to eliminate the unexpected. The price we pay for this convenience is loss of creativity.

Generative learning provides rewards.

If we think of ourselves as on a mental voyage, we can balance our attentions between where we've been and where we might go. Then curriculum becomes a device for giving perspective to our plans and potentials. It supports the development and use of theories and general strategies that can be applied across many instances and in varied circumstances.

What does it all mean?

Inquiry is natural to all of us as learners. There are no special talents or experiences we must possess; we are simply called upon to develop and make conscious use of what we do possess. Reflection is the primary vehicle for accomplishing this. We have to take charge of our thoughts, decisions and actions, to examine them and so be able to direct them. The fact that we can already so easily find, embedded as they are in our conventional curricula, engagements that are rich in inquiry potential is just one support for this argument.

Invitation

Reread the classroom vignette you wrote in chapter one and jot down several of the experiences from your curriculum that you value most — the pluses. Then make one or two wishes for your curriculum.

Pluses	Wishes

Conditions of inquiry

Janet's language story

During my first year in elementary school I didn't attempt to teach reading; I merely provided worksheets and comprehension questions to help the kids improve their skills. At the end of it I realized I knew nothing about how people read. I had heard that you become a better reader through reading, but I didn't know why, or have any idea what I might do to help kids become better readers.

I jumped at the chance to take a reading course at a local university. The instructor got me to look at what I did as a reader myself. Incredible! What I was asking of the children had almost nothing to do with what I did as I read. I decided to change my approach.

For instance, I organized a literature program where, in groups of five, my students tackled a novel. They were free to choose from the available titles, but I prepared them to choose by giving book talks and time to browse. I had also developed the habit of reading aloud from a chapter book after lunch and then getting them to talk about the book. "Talk to your neighbor about what connections you made with this chapter," I would say.

Given these experiences, the children had no problem keeping literature logs as they progressed in their group study. I simply asked them to write what connections they made each time they read a section of their book.

I also asked them to turn in their logs regularly. My major concern was to ensure that they were growing as readers. Of course I responded and used every chance to push them a bit. The kids kept logs throughout the year and I responded weekly. At the end of the year I collected all the logs and began a more formal study of them.

I found myself overwhelmed. So much data. After some reflection I decided to compare entries at the beginning of the year with those near the end, and so document the kinds of growth I saw occurring. Several other teachers and my university professor helped me develop a taxonomy for coding the kinds of comprehensive strategies we saw being employed. Some entries summarized what the children had read; others related parts of the stories to their lives; still others tied what they had read to other books. Some entries were evaluative, as in "I like this book because . . ."

About midway through this process I became interested in my own comments to the children — the ones I'd written in the margins. I was struck by changes in the tone and the content of those messages, changes that paralleled the way my own definition of reading was changing.

Fascinating! I'd begun by being curious about the ways children learn but ended up being fascinated by the way I myself had changed. I now realized how my own beliefs influence what I do for and to children. In my final course paper I reported on the taxonomy I had developed to code my responses to the children. It showed how my definition of reading had changed, and how that change had made a difference in the kinds of comprehension activities I was encouraging the kids to engage in.

Janet's story and the examples in the previous chapters were chosen to illustrate the central thesis of this book: that inquiry is the stuff classrooms should be made of. But what is genuine inquiry and under what conditions will it flourish? Neither of these questions is easy to answer, since any answer that is valid for you will include the specifics of your classroom, the pedagogical elements characteristic of your learning community. But we can talk about conditions for inquiry in meaningful ways, nevertheless, and that's what the rest of this chapter does. It sets out to help you answer this question for yourself: How do I recognize genuine inquiry?

Vulnerability

We've already stated our belief that all teachers work with theories: about the nature of children, the nature of learning and the nature of language. Even those who haven't (yet?) attempted to articulate their theories still have them — as do those who say they're not interested in theories, only in practical matters.

Teachers who decide the idea of inquiry might be useful in helping them understand what they and the children do in their classroom exhibit two sides of one coin. They know that they need to know what theory they're working with, and they know they need to put it to the question regularly. They are prepared to put their current theories at risk, to assume that at least one tenet of a particular theory is questionable, even if they don't at any one moment know which one. This uncertainty is one of the elements of vulnerability.

A second flows out of the need for inquirers to take a stance, to articulate a point of view. For instance, you may have had a flash of intuition that a long-held way of looking at a certain facet of writing holds no real water in your room full of active composers. But that intuition, perhaps followed by a second one about a possible alternative, may meet stiff initial resistance. Researchers (learners/inquirers) may not seek conflict, but they have no way of avoiding it when it comes. In fact, inquirers learn to be grateful for adversaries: opposition compels them to be clear about what it is they know that their opponents don't. It also helps them present the results of their inquiry in effective ways. But it's never easy.

When we begin to consider in more detail why we think research is "simply" a formalized version of the learning process, then the issue of vulnerability takes on depth. Feeling vulnerable has its difficult sides, of course, but we want to stress two things: first, that we're not talking simply about feeling vulnerable, and second, that we consider vulnerability a positive condition of inquiry (learning). Apart from spurring people on not to rest on previous laurels, vulnerability lies at the foundation of genuine human community. We'll come back to this later, but first a bit about the nature of learning as we see it.

Learning is connecting patterns.

Learning involves finding patterns that connect. Fortunately the human mind is programmed to find patterns and always accounts for reality in terms of patterns. For instance, you know that reading is learned by reading. Surround children with lots of reading materials, give them time to read, validate their being busy reading, and their reading improves. But this (recognized) pattern may not explain all you need to know about learning to read. You may need to learn more, link what you already know to new patterns that come your way. Learning involves finding new patterns and making connections between patterns where they didn't exist before. Growth — here another word for learning — entails finding ever more and ever broader patterns. While the process of finding new and broader patterns may be deliberately enriched, it can't ever be stopped except by death.

But how are new patterns identified and new links forged? For any learner the first step is to be sensitive to anomalies, either gaps between known patterns or unexpected events that don't fit in an existing pattern. For instance, Lawrence is surrounded by the same books as all the others in your class but his reading isn't improving. There's an anomaly here, one that catches your attention. You set out to learn more. You're concerned about Lawrence and need to discover the nature of the gap. You owe it to him professionally to find a new pattern so he can be helped. Anomalies focus attention and trigger the learning process.

Normally at this point, you (the learner) might do one of four things.

- You might decide to postpone any specific action.

Perhaps you don't know what to make of the anomaly, or what to do with it. In that case, doing nothing at the moment is not an inactive stance. You aren't ignoring the anomaly. You've recognized the different pattern and will be ready to observe further instances of it. If you do notice other instances, either at that time or some time later, then you'll take action. In the meantime the world of your classroom has already been changed through your awareness of this anomaly. Your stance as a learner has also been changed. There's a problem at hand. It keeps bothering you.

- You could, instead, deliberately collect more data — that is, make more observations.

Perhaps there are others in the class who are also not falling within the "readers improve through reading" pattern. Or you might notice that Lawrence is finally beginning to show signs of improving his reading. Or perhaps some explanation will present itself that isolates your original observation to a single case; for instance, Lawrence could simply have been ill on that day, or perhaps his life had been disturbed in some way, maybe by an unhappy situation at home or a bully on the block. Whatever the case, you feel uneasy until a satisfactory explanation is found.

Vulnerability is clearly present in the previous two courses of action, both in your feeling of vulnerability (professional ill-ease) and as a spur to action. But its intensity increases in the next two.

- You might decide to revise the initial pattern.

Perhaps it isn't enough to provide lots of good reading material, time to read and validation of the act of reading without also recognizing that reading must be done for real purposes. Perhaps Lawrence hasn't yet learned that reading is linked to personal agendas.

Revision of the pattern forces action in two directions. First, it brings learners face to face with the truth that learning does not and should not stop — ever. And because you've found one pattern imperfect, your sensitivity to potential weak links in other patterns will grow. Your watchfulness will increase. Second, as the example indicates, immediate new action is necessary — the provision of new elements in the learning environment.

- You might develop an entirely new pattern.

A fourth course of action creates an even greater degree of vulnerability. Perhaps an entirely new pattern is needed, one that explains and gives new meaning to both the old pattern and the new observation. Taken to sophisticated and comprehensive heights, a new pattern could take on the shape of a new paradigm, a radically different form or model of thinking about a reality like a classroom or a school.

Here risk-taking is elevated to great heights. The problem with a truly new paradigm (a fairly rare appearance in any culture) is that it usually employs new vocabularies and new ways of thought and these link uneasily to the vocabulary of former times. When two paradigms meet, we either have a mini Tower of Babel or two ships sailing past each other in the night. People find it difficult to talk to each other and make sense.

There's still one more side to the issue of vulnerability. Considering learning as inquiry invites new thinking about community, specifically the classroom learning community. While it's true that your thought-out patterns are what ought to be functioning in the classroom — you are the teacher, after all — you nevertheless need to be constantly open to the possibility that your students will present anomalies and require alternate patterns, and that makes you vulnerable.

Anomalies in your classroom are inevitable — they are the as yet unfulfilled needs of the children. Hear their voices and see their eyes. Here lies your greatest vulnerability, and the greatest spur to actions of inquiry and openness. More about this in the next section.

Community

A deep awareness of community is the second condition for learning as inquiry. This condition has its roots in the conviction that all knowledge is social. Everything worth knowing we know in community. Philosophers may want to argue the fine points of this statement, but as far as we're concerned, it's only when we hear someone speak that we can say, "We don't believe that" or "Here's what we think" or "I never thought about that before." We doubt prophets who don't gather followers in either the short or the long term. What any person claims to know must be confirmed by others in the human community.

For a long time our culture was firmly convinced that knowledge resided in individual minds. Facts were reality, and reality was out there, objective and sure, indisputable. Individual human minds would, after great and systematic effort, grasp it.

Some people still accord facts great honor, although fewer now than before. Some still give facts, once established, an indisputable life of their own, as if they could exist without regard for the feelings or the wishes of people. But more and more, both plain folk and learned scholars have become convinced that knowledge is situated in social contexts. After all, what is fact today was hypothesis yesterday. And what is fact today may be considered witchcraft tomorrow. Facts are not universal truths but rather socially and historically embedded concepts. In fact(!) even (and maybe we should say especially) learned physicists no longer believe in facts in the old way.

Only inquirers (researchers/learners) who believe in the social aspect of knowing and who put their belief into classroom practice can truly be trusted. It's only when ideas and insights are communicated — in other words, have become part of the community — that they become trustworthy and operational.

In the classroom community, widespread involvement is an important component of inquiry/learning. Knowledge generation should involve all affected members of the community from the beginning. Other people give us an opportunity to reflect on our own thinking and on the constructs we're using to make sense of the world. Their insights enrich and flesh out our narratives, help us to clarify our ideas and communicate more clearly. The strongest communities are built on differences, on a willingness to allow the different voices making up the community to be heard and listened to. It's by hearing unlike voices that the resources available in a community of learners become known and transformed. If everyone thinks alike there's no conversation. It's from difference that real conversations begin.

What all this means is that inquiry/research is, and ought to be, a subjective process that includes real subjects: living, active and reactive people. In the traditional model of research, key researchers don't give their subjects a real voice, nor a contributing stake. It's called "prioritizing the position of researchers." They treat everyone as an object, as a number to be worked on. Their work is called "objective" precisely because it is independent of specific subjects: thinkers, feelers, doers.

But we believe successful research must be collaborative. Researchers need informants to "co-labor" with them in the true sense of the word, and so help them outgrow their current selves. "Subjects" should have opportunities to bite, to catch the reseacher with his or her assumptions showing and pounce on the discovery. Research of this kind still presents results at the end of the process. But unlike the old style, it doesn't present results only at the end. Sharing with peers is an ongoing process: colleagues are involved from the start, used as informants and sounding boards, and urged to become owners themselves.

Moreover, for learning to be truly inquiry, an audit trail must be left, a set of research "vouchers" that are open to inspection. Key points in the ongoing process of inquiry must be available for scrutiny so that others can check and make their own judgments about the trustworthiness of the findings and, even more, of the conclusions.

The essential individualism of traditional research can easily result in researchers tricking themselves. After all, structurally they are talking to themselves, opening themselves and their conclusions up only at the end of the process — and then mostly in an adversarial posture. But in an inquiry/learning model, informants, trusted colleagues and alternate communication systems are in constant use. We use the image of "triangulating" knowing, borrowed from land surveyors and sailors who, by constantly changing their point of observation, have discovered all kinds of things about stars and other places. The image helps us keep in mind that there must be a constant, organic flow of information, an openness to surprises, to anomalies, even to paradoxes.

We believe that triangulation of knowing reduces the risk of tricking ourselves. One key to understanding research methodology is to think about what you might do to reassure yourself you're not being tricked — and that will increase the trustworthiness of your research. The beauty of it is that you'll find yourself doing a lot of very natural things that, when you get into the research literature, have fancy names. Often fancy names simply signal an "in group" mystique used to keep others out.

Generation of knowledge

Dewey gave us a name for the kind of inquiry that doesn't go beyond the here and now: "miseducation." A third condition of inquiry is that it must be generative — that is, it must propel new action. Good inquiry has a future about it.

Another, related, characteristic of generative research is that it's curricular. We want to emphasize the point that good research is part of a program of inquiry, an ongoing process of learning. "Curriculum" tells us that the future has been thought about, that the inquirer has had notions about the courses of action that should follow the results of current research. In our mind those courses of action had better be about "a better world." And researchers had better make sure that what they do and plan to do contributes to the building of such a world. As one of us is wont to say, "The function of inquiry is to give perspective."

By the same token, researchers need to understand that the world is not yet "better," that not everything being done is innocent. What research does says a lot about what the research is. Beyond the consideration that it may not have been worth the efforts of their involvement, researchers may have complex and not always articulated agendas. An evaluation of your own program of inquiry will need some reflection on the logical consequences of what will be done with the results.

Generative research must also result in theory. Earlier we made the point that professionals have no choice about whether or not to work from a theory base. Their only choice is whether or not to acknowledge their theory. Moreover, new theory must build on the current knowledge base. Researchers must remain informed and demonstrate how what they are doing contributes to the advancement of the field. (Advancement in this connection means new theory — new formulations of old patterns, or descriptions of new patterns.) Failing to meet this condition represents an anti-intellectual stance and violates the second condition for inquiry, namely that it be part of a community and connected to the work of other researchers, some perhaps no longer living. Both these considerations are hallmarks of real learning.

Since we are teachers, it's especially important that our inquiry build on what we know about the role of language and other sign systems within the overall patterns of knowing. Alternate communication systems — visual arts and dance, for instance — allow language learners the opportunity for triangulation as they take a new perspective on their knowing. Alternate communication systems not only enhance our knowing, but may also represent a self-correcting strategy within the research process.

Democracy

The fourth condition of inquiry must be rooted in a sense of what education is in a democracy. In a true democracy all voices are heard. Often schools, even those that take pride in being bulwark building blocks for democracy, silence certain voices. We think of children who bring to school only a non-English mother tongue, for instance, and we tell them that

English is the only language permitted in the classroom. Whole language is contributing classroom patterns that include hearing from students who have been silenced up to now.

We look for this characteristic in learning communities that proclaim themselves whole language. If whole language teachers are not drawing in the formerly silent, we must question what their program is really all about. In fact, we've been known to tell teachers that if they have a student they haven't heard from they should stop whatever they're doing and reorganize the day so that student is permitted a voice. This isn't abandoning curriculum but operationalizing it in a democracy.

Research too must be democratic. The role of inquiry is not to give one's own voice preference, or even to speak for others — you can never do that. Rather, the function of good research is to set up an environment where various voices can be heard. Good research, like good curriculum, invites participants to speak. Many teachers seem compelled to take one of two unproductive stances on this issue: they are either at the front of the classroom always being heard or at the back desperately trying to write themselves out of their own curriculum. Responsible inquirers understand it's by hearing new voices that new conversations and new actions proceed, and no voice must be overlooked or shut out, including that of the researcher!

A second aspect of this condition relates again to the point that all research has its base in theory. The responsibility of researchers is to make their assumptions and underlying beliefs explicit. There are several reasons for the exercise of this reponsibility. First, there ought not to be community agendas known only by a few, or only by the teacher. Classrooms heavily slanted towards performance on tests and exams, and with heavy emphasis on "academics," often have an agenda understood only by the teacher and a few top performers. The rest of the class is merely tolerated by the select few — and feels tolerated, and therefore often angry and resentful as well.

Often the very process of explicating one's assumptions about language, learning and curriculum in a research study is enough to launch a rethinking of them. And the experience of explicating your own assumptions will help you understand what other researchers have done and what their results mean or don't mean. Educational inquiry would be greatly improved if inquirers took as a given that probably at no point in time do they fully understand the reasons for the positions they hold, nor the consequences of what their current actions will be. This puts them on guard and establishes a readiness to spot anomalies they need to question and new directions they need to move in.

A third side has us recognize again that scholarship is not always innocent. A key question to ask is who is empowered and who is disempowered by specific inquiry/learning, a point implicit in the previous example of an "academic" classroom. Educational inquirers have a responsibility to make their politics explicit. Not to take a position is to maintain the status quo — to keep both those who are empowered and those who are disempowered in place. There's no neutral position.

Yet this emphasis on democracy isn't to say that all knowledge is of equal worth. Often reseachers assume that, but we think it's nonsense. There's nothing to learn by testing weak hypotheses. Learners grow by testing their best ideas. The last few years have made it abundantly clear that some otherwise popular theories of reading are less powerful than others. It's stupid to treat a faulty theory as equal to a more powerful model. There's nothing to learn by pursuing faulty theory, for at best you will merely confirm what you already know. What is worse, you'll have wasted your time on not growing.

Reflexivity

This final condition for sound inquiry refers to the ability to use yourself and others as instruments for your learning. It means that you constantly look at what people, yourself and others, do in the act of learning X or Y. Reflexivity actually provides a chronological starting point in the form of a stance of more or less permanent curiosity, the door to genuine inquiry.

But you need to be more than superficially curious, to not limit yourself to the level of intuition. When the principles of good teaching are left at an intuitive level they are beyond consciousness and hence beyond examination. Articulating what you understand intuitively allows you to use intuition as a basis for growth and learning. Following awareness of an anomaly, for instance, articulating intuition typically produces a new hypothesis for testing.

Language plays a key role in reflexivity. It allows each of us to name our world. The minute we label a chunk of experience, we make that experience public. But the beauty of language is that it's not only public, it's social. Language didn't develop because of one language user, but two. To put something into language is to make that something social and a potential contribution to the welfare of others. New ideas made public help thought collectives (classrooms) grow.

This process of naming experience makes interesting things happen. By putting our experience into language we take distance from it, transform it into something that can be turned upside down, stepped back from, twirled around and studied, by ourselves and others. And we can use what others say about our experience to judge the adequacy of our naming process, as well as of the concept that encompasses our experience. In short, we can begin to interrogate and understand the very constructs we use to make sense of the world. To be able to understand and unpack these constructs in terms of their historical, political and social origins is a necessary step in becoming a reflexive researcher.

Often researchers feel that the key to better research, new insights, improved curriculum, or whatever, is a new test, a new curricular package, a new statistical procedure. This is wrong. In the final analysis the key to becoming a good researcher is the ability and willingness to use yourself as an instrument for your own learning. Understanding your role and how you can use language for your own learning is a necessary condition for becoming an inquirer/learner. (See again Janet's story.)

What we are saying is that you should never engage in the inquiry/learning process on behalf of, or for the sake of, the learning of others. Learning is what learners do. The focus has to be on your own learning and what you are interested in learning about. And don't be afraid of any interest you might have. Being human entitles you to an inquiring voice, and it's from asking new questions — and old questions for which current answers seem unsatisfactory — that real learning emanates. Count yourself in, as you are. If what you do has positive effects on the learning of others (and it will!), consider that a side-benefit of the inquiry process but not the prime focus. Be good to yourself. All learning begins as a form of egotism.

A second aspect of reflexivity we've touched upon already. Researchers sit inside their research, are personally part of the research context. Researchers don't stand outside the text, cool observers whose private thoughts and feelings zig-zag among impersonal research problems. Because of their presence, contexts will change. How often has a visitor to your classroom promised to be "invisible"? Polite but impossible. Any classroom is changed by a visitor. In the same way any inquiry is made unique by the person or persons who inquire. Don't delude yourself into feeling you can ignore your role in the inquiry process. Researchers are more truthful (and better off) acknowledging the fact that they've had an impact on the inquiry setting.

The same holds true for reporting results. Traditional research reports make "objective" sounds, with lots of passive phrases and impersonal pronouns. We talked about this recently with reference to an airline announcement we'd heard: "As part of our overall policy, this plane has been selected as a non-smoking flight." The truth is, of course, that in view of the current public outcry against smoking, the top executives of the airline, a group of very specific people with real names and families, made a policy decision to make most of their domestic flights smokefree. Next, middle executives, lower down the ladder but also with specific names, decided that this particular flight would be one of those. It isn't true that "this plane has been selected." It is true that someone has selected this plane.

Too often the researcher's or writer's voice is neutralized, leaving an "it" or a "one" in charge. A much more honest approach is to acknowledge your own voice and show how your personal view of the world has shaped the research results. Moreover, whenever possible, collaborators must be permitted to speak for themselves. It's impossible to speak for others.

Summary

Vulnerability, a sense of community, the view that knowledge is generative, democratic and reflexive: these are the hallmark conditions for learning and research, as we see it. And it must have become clear to you in reading this chapter how intertwined we feel these five conditions are. Ripping any one from the context of learning will damage the rest.

If that sounds forbidding, here are two bits of comfort. First, the longer teachers embrace a whole language approach in their classrooms, the more they drift, naturally and holistically, toward the conditions of true inquiry. Second, many teacher support groups, like TAWL, already incorporate them. This chapter is not an announcement of something unknown. Rather, it's a description and clarification of something already emerging.

Invitation

Think back to your curricular wish and list the things you think you already know. Then list what you think you want to learn and what you plan to do to meet each of the conditions of inquiry.

	I know	I want to learn	I plan to do
Vulnerability			
Community			
Generation of knowledge			
Democracy			
Reflexivity			

Invitations and encouragements

Not that anyone would notice today, but long ago one of us joined a Weight Watchers group and was a fairly diligent member. After the first week he and the other initiates into the program weighed in. The group as a whole had lost 39 pounds, but one member had gained two. The director asked what had happened. The response was classic: "I took a week to think about it."

Don't take a week. Start implementing your curricular wish now.

This chapter contains a number of accounts of how others began, stories that exhibit the principles and ideas discussed in the previous chapters. They all have their origins in real events, in generative situations, and come out of our own professional lives.

Story 1: Teacher support groups

Every Friday evening Debbie telephones Mark, whose school is a considerable distance from hers, across a huge metropolitan city. They talk, sometimes for hours, about their students' projects, the effect of warmer weather on the concentration powers of ten-year-olds, a poem written by Jake ("Jake the Jock," also former school bully), their own families and personal welfare. Mark asks about Debbie's students as if he knows them intimately. Debbie checks out Mark's precarious relationship with his principal. They discuss articles in the latest professional journals and share titles of children's books. Debbie and Mark have formed a teacher support group of two.

Barbara's support group is much different. Once a month Barbara packs the trunk of her car with a box of professional books and heads for her TAWL meeting (Teachers Applying Whole Language). The group fills a room and often spills into the hall of a local elementary school. When Barb arrives with her "books for sale," Janice is setting up "books to borrow" on a table in the hall. Professional and children's books can be bought and borrowed and the action is brisk. Other members are busy arranging the meeting room and setting up refreshments.

The group includes teachers, administrators and librarians. There are first year teachers and some who have recently retired, teachers from both private and public schools, from preschool level up to college, including teacher educators — anyone interested in whole language learning and teaching. Some have been members of the group since it started with six teachers almost a decade ago. For some this is their first meeting. They're here to listen to each other's voices.

The food and companionship refresh. Kittye starts the meeting with calendar announcements: time of the next meeting, deadline for the newsletter, date for a board meeting, information about the annual conference sponsored by this TAWL group.

Five previously designated members share "language stories and literacy lessons":

- Examples of dialectic journals from a grade 10 literature class.
- A progress report on literature study groups in a "learning disabilities" class.
- Mention of a new Virginia Hamilton book.
- A show of classroom-published books by first-graders. One member begins drafting a letter of thanks-for-sharing to the children and passes it around for members to add their personal thanks.
- A "good news, bad news" story: second-grader Jody wrote his first story, only to have his dad disapprove of his invented spelling and non-standard grammar.

The sharing lasts about an hour and includes some unplanned offerings: for instance, an enthusiastic account from Virginia of her children's enactment of Beverly Cleary's *Remarkable Ramona*. Jody's story is picked up again and two members promise to talk more with the concerned teacher.

After a short break the members meet in small groups to discuss professional articles selected earlier. The structure of the groups encourages wide-open discussion, helped along by a convenor and a note-taker. Some groups get right down to business, others take an extra minute or two at the refreshments. Jody's concerned teacher is still the center of one small group. But soon several concentrated meetings of minds and hearts are in full swing.

Careful observation of the discussions reveals two agendas. First, these teachers express and discuss a variety of research questions that well up out of the literature they're studying. But just as importantly, they live through the group process. They want to feel as their students do when they're involved in literature study groups. They want to experience how discussions come alive, how inquiry becomes urgent. They want to learn how to make a heartfelt response to another learner. They pay careful attention to themselves when they hold a minority point of view and feel unsupported. They want to learn how to develop self-evaluation (How did I do?) and group evaluation (How did we do?).

This session lasts about 45 minutes and comes to a reluctant halt only at Kittye's insistence. Each group reports, sharing the contents of the literature and individual transactions with it, but focusing also on the group process: what went right and what went wrong (the anomalies). Suggestions and research questions for the next meeting are agreed upon.

As usual, the unwritten 10 o'clock rule is bent slightly as members exchange last-minute notes, wish each other well, tidy the room and head for home, tired but inspired.

The pattern

Most TAWL groups begin with a handful of teachers who want to share the practical theories and theoretical practices of whole language. Meeting agendas often include:

- a sharing of writings, their own and those of their students
- a sharing of professional literature, theme research and classroom writing workshops
- a sharing of children's literature
- a sharing of burdens, which usually turns into inquiry: What can I do? Where do I go for help? What are my options?

As groups get larger they become a bit more formal, presenting strategies, reviewing articles and sharing various research projects. Often presentations become dress rehearsals for state and provincial conferences, or for IRA and NCTE meetings. TAWL group presentations are ideal forums for seeking and receiving valuable critiques by sympathetic colleagues — who may be front and center next time.

These groups never miss an opportunity to invite guests who happen to be in town: an author, a whole language teacher from another city, a knowledgeable publisher. And they don't forget the home front either: a junior poet will come to tell how school has helped and hindered her work, a successful drama and music teacher from a school nearby will share "how to" ideas, a person who met some British teachers while on holidays will describe the situation over there.

Large or small, teacher support groups provide teachers with opportunities to share, brag and complain. But also, and most of all, to inquire.

Story 2: Experience centers

Pam spent two and a half weeks of her summer taking a graduate course in reading at the local university. She and 25 others explored recent research in language and curriculum. They each had to reflect on the strengths and weaknesses of their own curriculum, make a wish about some aspect of it, and develop it into a curriculum resource book.

The organization of the course embodied a whole language curriculum model called "authoring cycle." Each learner would contribute directly to the creation of the course curriculum and help collaborate to achieve its realization. All the course engagements were to be potential resources for the curricular wishes. During the course, Pam and her colleagues learned to see themselves as curriculum researchers and to appreciate the power of collaboration. They learned to trust the thrust of individual experiences and perspectives as contributors to a group effort.

At the end of the course the professor asked the teachers if they would enjoy collaborating in the fall with undergraduates who were taking a language education course. Small groups would visit the teacher's classroom for a half day each week and collaborate in implementing the teacher's wish, now recorded in the curriculum resource book. Pam immediately accepted this invitation and arrangements were made for 10 undergraduates to become collaborative members of her classroom that fall.

Pam wanted to replay with her own fourth-grade class the scenario of that summer course she'd enjoyed so much. So she reserved a one-hour time block twice each week for what she called "invitations." On Wednesday she would be with the students by herself, and on Friday the university collaborators would join. Invitations would include a wide range of open-ended activities offered to both small groups and individuals. For instance, uninterrupted reading or writing, literature discussion circles, authors' circles and editing tables would fit into a one-hour block. And so would "experience centers."

Experience centers would include engagements planned to highlight a relationship, process or concept for analysis. Pam's purpose was to encourage alternative thinking, based on these criteria:

- The engagements should be accessible to people of varied experience and language flexibility.
- They should be challenging to all learners in the class, including herself.

These experiences would also build the foundation for a long-term strategy, namely to create a classroom in which teacher and students become co-learners/researchers. To begin with Pam developed three experience centers to develop the concept of perspective.

New perspectives

A researcher has to be able to see familiar things in a new way. Take, for instance, the traditional formalized perspectives on the world that we usually call subjects: social studies, mathematics, biology, etc. Each field has developed tools and methods suited to the kinds of questions under study, but Pam wanted to encourage her students to establish new and varied perspectives.

She put together a collection of pictures: an urban street scene with a policeman talking to a young child, a partially constructed home with workmen on the roof, a farmer plowing a field, a doctor's office with a patient receiving a shot, and others. She invited the students, in pairs, to select one photograph and generate questions a variety of people from different walks of life (economist, historian, teacher, mathematician, chemist) might ask of that setting and situation. She encouraged them to make additional visits to the center to explore the varied scenes, develop a selection of questions for each picture and record them on paper.

Varied perspectives

Sets of trade books offer a way to experience various perspectives on a single theme. Pam assembled several sets and put a blank log with each set, an invitation on its cover. Following are three samples of book sets, including the theme, the book titles and the invitation.

Ways to see

Alphabetics, Suse MacDonald
Animals Should Definitely Not Wear Clothing, Judith Barrett
Fish Is Fish, Leo Lionni
Just Me, Marie E. Ets
The Pain and the Great One, Judy Blume
The Painter and the Wild Swans, Claude Clement
The Paper Bag Princess, Robert N. Munsch

Quick as a Cricket, Audrey Wood
Roald Dahl's Revolting Rhymes, Roald Dahl
The Snail Spell, Joanne Ryder

"Each of these books gives an opportunity to consider something from more than one perspective. Record some of the perspectives you consider."

Changing scenes

The Changing City, Jorg Muller
The Changing Countryside, Jorg Muller
The Little House, Virginia Lee Burton
New Providence, Renata von Tscharner and Ronald Lee Fleming
The Story of a Main Street, John S. Goodall
Venice: Birth of a City, Piero Ventur

"Humans change environments over time. Hunt for and record what you see as the major causes of change."

Castles

Castle, David Macaulay
Learning About Castles and Palaces, Ruth Shannon Odor
Life in a Castle, Althea
The Tower of London, Leonard Everett Fisher

"What can you learn about medieval life from the architectural design of castles?"

Pam encouraged her students to form into small groups of three to six and select a book set that interested them. Group members browsed through the books, read some or all and shared observations. The invitation was meant to (and did!) focus attention. Group members recorded their observations in the log so they were available to groups using that set later.

Deeper perspectives

Literature study often calls for the examination of one text in relationship with another. In order to draw useful comparisons, learners have to be able to consider both the surface and the deep structures of the stories being considered. Pam wanted to help her students see beyond the obvious perspectives to deeper, more inclusive relationships. The following pairs of books, and others, offered excellent opportunities for compare/contrast analysis of deep-structure relationships:

Cinderella and *Prince Cinders* (main character a male, modern setting)

Goldilocks and *Deep in the Forest* (a wordless picture book in which the traditional roles are reversed when a young bear invades a human family's home while they are taking a walk in the forest)

Working in twos, the students selected a book pair. In some cases both read both books, in some cases each read one. Following the reading, they told the stories to each other, looking for similarities and differences. As the discussion developed and they began to give weight to the various relationships they noted, they recorded their observations on a chart. Even more exciting was later comparing the different charts produced by different students for the same book pair.

Results

Over the weeks, as the members of the class made their invitation-time choices and participated in experience centers, Pam looked for evidence of their growing ability and inclination to generate questions. She wanted to encourage conscious recognition of questions as they occurred, and invited individuals who generated them to pursue them. When Nadine, for instance, thought she recognized a relationship between Cinderella and Yeh Sheen, a book she'd been given for Christmas, she was encouraged to bring her book in and create a new paired book set.

When the students became curious about the personal and professional lives of the undergraduate collaborators who joined them for a half day each week, Pam suggested a pen-pal exchange which evolved into a six-week focused study. The theme of the study was "Getting to Know Someone." Many of the questions, tools and procedures the inquirers used were those anthropologists use as well, although the students had not yet learned the fancy names for them.

Pam's intent had found clearly positive response. The experience centers were becoming real inquiry engagements, challenging to both the adults and the children in the class. It's evident that these kinds of engagements do invite children to create and pursue their own inquiries.

Story 3: Planning to plan

Every education undergraduate expects that major and complex course assignment known as "the unit." That's when friends and relatives are called upon for anything they have or know about "The Sudan," "The Northern Climes" or "The Life Cycle of the Butterfly." Maps and globes, tables and charts, books and articles, lists of films and videos, pictures and filmstrips, magazines (what would we do without the *National Geographic*?) and any artifacts from close or distant resource people are collected and placed in the unit box. Methods classes — language arts, social studies, science — are all grist for the unit mill.

Take "The Encyclopedia," for instance, assigned in a language arts course and memorable, perhaps, because the person in question still has some real doubts about its usefulness. She studied and collected types of encyclopedias. She copied excerpts from different editions. She located a filmstrip on how encyclopedias are made. She wrote a series of six carefully constructed lesson plans, including multiple worksheets, on the use of the encyclopedia. And because the unit box wasn't filled to the brim this resourceful person cheated and added a bit of information about other resource books as well. Of course she also produced a scholarly analysis on how a study of the encyclopedia could fit into Bloom's Taxonomy.

The use of prefabricated materials tells a great deal about what a teacher believes about teaching and learning, about teachers and learners, about curriculum development, about the culture of the students, including their homes and families. Whole language teachers know that materials found in unit boxes can be helpful, but that on their own they can never cause learning and teaching to come alive, make children and teachers enthusiastic participants in research and inquiry, or even necessarily add authenticity to the curriculum. It's imperative in using them to consider the interests and strengths of the students and to evaluate appropriate inquiry strategies. "Planning to plan" is what we call these activities.

Let's look at "planning to plan theme studies" as an example. We want to show how mistaken and naive is the view that whole language teachers just "groove on kids," have nothing clearly in mind before the students tell them what they want to do, and have no use for pre-planning. Whole language teachers are open to the voices of all learners, do value students' abilities and don't set curriculum in motion before learners validate its content and strategies. But doing all this makes them work very hard at planning to plan, to prepare a basis for their invitations to students and to take into account all the resources available for curricular construction.

Planning to plan theme studies

The following model might help you see the various aspects of planning to plan. Of course the very nature of this strategy invites you to alter it to suit your own needs.

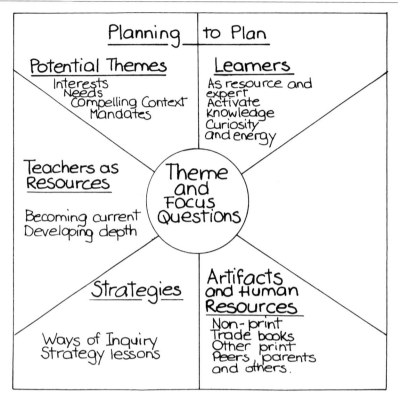

There are a number of potential topic sources. Clearly the first ones are themes you know to be of genuine interest to the students, and ones they honestly need to know something about. Your own life and background are a second source. Because Nancy is a pilot and her enthusiasm is contagious, her students are inevitably interested in aspects of piloting. Compelling current events are sure to engage learners: a political election, a tornado nearby, the excavation for a supermarket across the street, a new student from Thailand, spring "bustin' out all over" — all themes worth consideration.

Less motivating are those topics that must be studied for reasons outside the lives of the learners — usually because standardized tests or textbooks direct the curriculum. Mandates from the district, state or province must be evaluated for their authenticity. Teachers sometimes face threats to their jobs if the mandated curriculum isn't "covered," and students shouldn't be made to look bad on mandated tests. Sometimes teachers have to make decisions about how these mandates can be handled in a supportive way, or subsumed (there are a lot of ways to "cover" the mandates) under something more appropriate and appealing to the learners.

Those learners become the next crucial focus for planning a theme. What did your former students like for themes? Where did they emerge as researchers and inquirers? What themes generated new knowledge and promoted personal and social learning and growth? In other words, which themes could you replay? There's a danger here of falling into the "golden oldie" trap: if it worked well before, we'll do it again. But the curriculum can't be in place before the learners are in place. The voices of the new kids on the block must be heard.

To find out about your learners, set the inquiry up in such a way that they see themselves as resources not only for their own research, but for the other inquirers in the community of learners. To know your students is to know when and where to help them build on their own background ("You know a lot of exciting and valuable stuff about bee-keeping"), to activate available knowledge ("Can you give Ralph a few minutes of your time to tell him about your dad's 18-wheeler for his study on transportation?"), and to stimulate curiosity and energy ("I've found a little experiment on capillary action that might fit into your research, if you're interested").

"Planning to plan" encourages teachers to take a closer look at their own contribution. This self-examination will spur them on to become more clearly resource persons, by watching for potential themes and looking at possible topics in depth. Knowledgeable teachers who themselves research and study see possibilities for the explorations of other learners, suggest side trips that may prove exciting, and in general brighten and enrich the tapestry.

The unit box as depository of resources shouldn't be tossed aside. In addition to the artifacts, all the materials stashed in the unit box are evaluated with interest and enthusiasm: the non-print resources, the trade books and possibly even some textbooks. Nevertheless, human resources, including other students, parents and acknowledged enthusiasts and experts, are the most valuable.

Another facet of planning to plan is asking questions about learning and teaching. What strategies are appropriate to the content of the themes? If the inquiry has to do with history, what are the kinds of questions historians ask? If it's about patterns and designs, what questions do weavers and other artisans ask?

One section of the model has been left blank: it's specifically for you. We invite you to consider and jot down what you think is necessary for you to hear all the voices within your community of learners.

Story 4: Pen-pals

Jan's second-graders loved writing to children in Mexico City. Each time letters arrived the classroom was charged with electricity, but unfortunately letters arrived only three times during the entire year. Jan's original idea had been that the children would research their writing over time, evaluate their own growth and talk about how they were moving along in their ability to communicate with someone they'd never met. But three letters didn't provide enough opportunities for them to learn about themselves, much less about strangers.

Lois knew about Jan's frustration. For her undergraduate course in literacy and learning she regularly brought in examples of children's writing and drawing, showed video tapes of classrooms in action and asked her students to listen to recordings of children reading. Her students, future teachers, learned from these experiences, but Lois too felt that something was missing. They often talked to her about their fears of student teaching, and even more about the day they would assume full responsibility for a classroom.

One day Lois and her students were talking about ways of getting to know children when one of them pulled from his pocket a letter written by his kid sister. The others began to ask him all kinds of questions about his sister, genuine questions that grew out of a real desire to know. They were curious. They had an intuition that there was a relationship between the data in the letter and their need to find ways of learning important things about the students they would eventually have. And so Lois suggested the idea of exchanging letters with the children in Jan's class.

Jan and Lois, members of the same TAWL group, invited a third member, Sawyer, a grade six teacher, to join them in the pen-pal adventure. Quickly the writing, the friendships and the learning got under way. Lois and the undergraduates decided that pen-palling was an important way to learn and they mustn't take the project lightly. During the course of a semester they hoped to send seven letters and receive seven in return — enough to provide a good deal of data to analyze. Over time they hoped to see advancement in both the children's writing and their own.

The adult writers began to research what they needed to know about seven- and eleven-year-old children in order to have a good pen-pal friendship. They asked what their colleague wrote to his sister and what got the most productive responses. For the first time they felt that children could inform them. They wanted to hear their voices. These undergraduates were beginning to feel like researchers, like learners, like teachers.

They shared their first letters with their study partners — to give themselves a chance to revise and relieve their minds about setting a bad example for the children. They didn't want any non-standard spelling and grammar to creep in. Before they took their letters to Lois and Sawyer, they shared them once more in class, taking notes on what they heard the others say, things to think about for next time.

Lois suggested that the undergraduates make a copy of their letters before sending them so that as the correspondence continued they would be able to see what the children were responding to, what generated spirited conversation, how they changed in their understanding of their pen-pals and how their relationship with the children grew.

It was a magic day when the letters arrived in the second and sixth grade classrooms. The uninterested pored over the pages, the lonely found a friend, the non-readers read, the disruptive were captivated. And every learner became a writer in response.

As the semester progressed, the friendships grew. Jan and her second-graders valued the experience and saw it as an integral part of their curriculum. The children eagerly wrote to their friends not only personal narratives but the curricular narrative of the classroom. The future teachers learned about social studies, science and math projects, acted as resources for research endeavors, wrote stories with their pals, exchanged jokes and shared secrets.

But by the seventh week it became apparent that the letters from the sixth-graders didn't reflect the same joy and care. Lois and the undergraduates were concerned and began to research the problem. Was it the content of their letters that failed to inspire? Was it that eleven-year-olds don't care much for pen-palling? They worked harder to make their letters interesting, to give of themselves, to refrain from interrogating their new friends, to invite shared ownership of the activity.

Week nine brought more short, perfunctorily written notes from the sixth-graders. It was time to find out what the problem was. In their next letters they asked their pen-pals to tell them what they thought of their correspondence. Direct inquiry lead to direct answers: "I don't have time to write." "I have to take my letter home to finish it or write it during play time." "I don't know for sure what is okay to put in my letters."

Lois invited Sawyer, Jan and two undergraduates to meet for a discussion about the project to share questions, comments and concerns. Unable to contain her enthusiasm, Jan spoke first. She started by telling about the impact the pen-pal project had had on her, the children and their curriculum. It had become a generating strategy that encompassed all the language arts. She told of times when the children referred to information in their pals' letters as they worked on their content area projects. The children read the letters they received over and over and shared them with others. The parents loved the project. For some this was the first time their children voluntarily shared anything from school. Two parents told Jan that their children had asked permission to write letters to family members.

Sawyer got the point. Pen-palling was part of the second grade curriculum. It wasn't something hastily added on to it: "If you're good and finish your 'real work' you can write your letter." Pen-palling was an inquiry in which the children moved from being learner to teacher and back again. It was an authentic engagement, one the children knew was valued since time and effort were devoted to it.

Finally, the undergraduates shared with Jan and Sawyer what they were learning from the letters. They glowed as they responded to questions. When these future teachers reported on the meeting to their undergraduate classmates they talked of the "theoretical stance" of the teachers, of the necessity of "curricular sensitivity." And they closed by saying that they would never forget this professional experience.

The semester wound to a close. The pen-pals met. The children were delighted that their friends brought with them all their letters. "That's my first letter. I was really young when I wrote that. I didn't even know how to spell *adventure!*"

On the next page are two pen-pal letters from Shannon, a first-grader whose teacher is a member of a TAWL group in Missouri. In her analysis of the first one, written in September, Shannon's pen-pal, Merri, noted:

". . . she used writing conventions such as top to bottom and left to right. She used small circles to help her space her words. She showed that she was a risk-taker by using invented spelling such as *WAT* for *wait, MET* for *meet, LEC* for *like,* and by using letter sounds to spell: *PPL* for *pen-pal* and *W* for *went.* Shannon is using prior knowledge of letter names and sounds to do this. Shannon's use of writing is interactional and personal. She used her writing to build her relationship with me in a positive way.

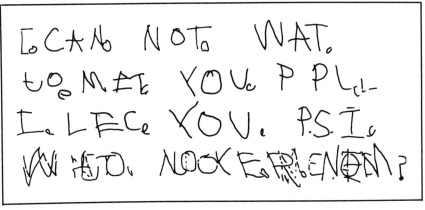

(I can not wait to meet you penpal. I like you. P.S. I w to nooke r nom?)

(Dear Merri, Thanksgiving time is coming fast. It's cold. We made shape books. I got messed up a little but I arranged it a little. I like any stickers. I like unicorns. I will send a picture of me. When I was in kindergarten we dressed up like Indians for Thanksgiving.)

She may have been influenced by my envelope as she drew a stamp in the upper right hand corner of her letter and wrote a *P.S.* in answer to my question. After the *P.S.* she copied from my letter. The question mark may have been an acknowledgment of my question or an indication that she didn't know how to spell the words."

Of the second letter, written in November, Merri noted:

". . . In Shannon's sixth letter the content changes. Previously her writing had been influenced mostly by things I had written. Here she writes about a school project: shape books. I speculate that she was encouraged by the fact that I had modeled something from her last letter. In keeping with the holiday, she wrote about Thanksgiving (word was on the board). As I did in my previous letter, she mentions the weather. Shannon attempts to give me information I asked for in my last letter — *tell me what you like.* She started to write, *I look Lille* but decided instead to say *I will SanD a pajR av me.* For the first time in her letters Shannon uses a contraction — an exclamation mark in place of an apostrophe. She knows some punctuation is needed but isn't sure what kind. Shannon continues to use more lower case letters. She still erases and revises her writing, showing that she is actively engaged in self-correction."

In reflecting on the semester Lois considered possible alternatives and alterations. She realized that she too should have had a pen-pal, perhaps a teacher, perhaps one of the children. Sawyer asked Jan to meet with him on a regular basis to talk about curriculum. The sixth-graders and the second-graders decided to bring pen-palling even closer to home: they would pen-pal with each other.

The pen-palling strategy prompted the inquiring voices of teachers, students, student teachers, teacher educators and, to some extent, parents. Within this teaching/learning engagement the curriculum, including evaluation, was shaped and made real.

Story 5: Field experience

Sharon writes:

It's been a long time since I sat in methods courses. I remember little about them — only a vague feeling of unreality and boredom, of going through the motions. It was hard to imagine myself in a real classroom with real children. There were no field experiences before student teaching at the small college I attended — a few weeks of student teaching and then sink or swim in the real world. What I'd learned in college and the demands of a real classroom didn't come together for me and I felt totally unprepared for teaching.

During student teaching there was little opportunity to have the type of relationship with my cooperating teacher that could have helped bridge the gap and make it a memorable intellectual experience. No wonder it took me nearly 10 years to discover that teaching is really a process of inquiry.

During doctoral studies at Indiana University I was given the opportunity to teach a reading and language arts methods course. I decided to explore a different model of teacher education, one that would improve the quality of teacher education classes and also support classroom teachers in their attempts to remain current.

First I met with the university's field placement director to discuss the one morning each week my students would spend in a local elementary classroom. I requested placement for them and myself at the school where I had taught fourth grade for four years. I still knew most of the teachers, as well as the principal, new since I taught there. My request was granted.

Next, I met with the principal. He was excited about the possibility of having his teachers and my students work more closely together than had been the case in the past. He himself had an interest in teaching undergraduate education. We decided to team teach my course, and on site rather than at the university. My students would be placed with teachers who volunteered for the project. Volunteers would be given Friday afternoons to attend the course and work with "their" undergraduate to research some topic of common interest. We called these collaborative efforts "learner projects."

Stephanie and Sara decided to study invented spelling. They wanted to assure themselves that children who write each day naturally move towards more conventional spelling. They developed a computer program for tabulating and recording words in each story. Midway through the year it dawned on them that this information was too important to keep to themselves, so they gave printouts to the children. Now each composer could see what words they had no trouble spelling and what words were problematic, as well as how their vocabulary and spelling competence was growing. The children were encouraged to use their printouts as their personal dictionaries.

At the end of the year, Stephanie and Sara reported on how the children used these dictionaries and shared them with each other. The results were clear: children grew as spellers without having a formal spelling program in their classroom, certainly without reducing the language arts curriculum to spelling. A fellow teacher argued with the report. "You do have a formal spelling program," she insisted, though she agreed it wasn't a "conventional" one. The presenters thanked her. They agreed that this was a much better way to talk about their program.

Kristina and Trish decided to introduce the authoring cycle into their curriculum. They began by simply providing opportunities for the children to write each day. They were amazed with the effects and devoted their first progress report to showing how much more the children were producing than they had been at the start of the year. They argued that the average length of stories had gone from four to nine sentences and that an analogous jump had occurred in vocabulary use.

They found most fascinating the "Authors' Circle," a time when four or five authors got together to share their writing and get feedback from one another. They decided to make their formal project the study of the kinds of support the children offered each other. They transcribed the audio tapes of these sessions and developed a taxonomy for coding the different kinds of suggestions and other forms of support. Theirs was an exciting adventure, as their concluding comment of their final presentation shows: "So, we started out as sceptics and now find ourselves as advocates of process writing. We have one recommendation for other teachers: trust the process and trust the kids. We know that the kids in our classroom became better readers as a result of their experience in writing. That's our next project."

I could go on. Some pairs focused on ways to improve reading comprehension; others on the value of good literature in a reading and writing program. At the final joint session of the course, the professor asked Stephanie, "What did you really learn about teaching? Why was this whole experience valuable to you? What could I say to convince the university that other students should have similar experiences?"

Stephanie paused a moment and said, "Well, I just see teaching differently now. I see it as learning. I was always excited about teaching, now I'm ecstatic. The other day I was talking with some friends who are in old-fashioned methods courses. It made me realize that I feel connected. I feel like I am a real teacher. They are still pretending. They are like outsiders looking in. I feel like an insider."

Sara responded to the same questions this way: "Well, it was different for me too. I think the fact that we were both learners together made a big difference. Stephanie and I have a professional relationship. I'm sure we are going to be friends for life. I didn't feel like I had to be Stephanie's teacher. We could be learners together and that fact alone made the experience a much richer one than I had ever had before. I think I even understand what you all mean when you use the term collaboration now."

Sharon concludes her account this way:

This is my story. Isn't it interesting that it's full of stories by others. Their stories became and shaped mine. That's how I understand collaboration to work.

Story 6: Writer's guild

"What's the matter? Why are you crying?"

"I'm stuck," said Cindy, a resource room teacher, between sobs. "This is never going to make sense. I'm stupid. Everybody else is writing and none of this makes sense to me."

"Nonsense. Stop crying. You're not stuck as long as you have me. Remember, anyone can intimidate a language user. We're here to support each other, make each other look better than we would if we worked alone."

"Oh, don't start that philosophical stuff! It won't work."

"Enough of that! Start writing about your frustration and why you're frustrated. Stop thinking you're unique. Everyone who's ever tried to do research feels the same way you're feeling. I've never been involved in a study when, after I get all the data collected and sit down to write, I don't secretly pray for a fire. Everyone would say, 'Oh, it's too bad he lost all his data' and I would inwardly smile. It's hard seeing patterns. Remember, anyone can see chaos; it takes looking a long time to see patterns that make a real difference. Begin with where you are, don't fight it. Your frustration is part of the process, capitalize on it. Be thankful you care enough to cry. Be human. Start from your own experience. Once you have some of that on paper we'll have an authors' circle and you'll be surprised how far you are."

With this conversation I left Cindy. She started writing. When she came to the author's circle I reminded her fellow teacher/researchers, members of a "writers' guild" for teachers engaged in doing research in their classrooms, that we were there to make each other look better than we could look by ourselves. The first requirement was that we listen, the second that we receive what had been written, the third that we let Cindy tell us what kind of help she wanted, and the fourth that we follow through with suggestions that she could take down and use or not, as she saw fit.

Cindy finished her project, I'm happy to report. Bobby, the student she was working with, was a particularly recalcitrant learner. Each time she asked him to write, he would string a series of *p*'s and *b*'s and *d*'s together. When she asked him to read what he'd written he would tell a beautiful story. The problem was that what he said the story said and the print he wrote showed little one-to-one correspondence.

And nothing she did seemed to help. In utter frustration Cindy said one day, "Do you see how I can read Matt's story? He writes so the letters and sounds go together and I can figure out what he's trying to say. When are you going to write like that? What can I do to help you?"

Bobby thought for a minute. "Probably," he said, "you could write the alphabet down for me on a piece of paper and tape it to my desk."

Cindy did this and lo and behold Bobby's writing started to take shape. Instantly he was able to create invented spellings an adult could read!

During the year Cindy explored this problem further. She finally concluded that Bobby simply didn't have a visual memory for letters, as most children do. Left on his own he would write only *p*'s and *b*'s and *d*'s. But if he had access to the alphabet while he was writing he could produce *KAT* for *cat*, *ONSAPONTIM* for *Once upon a time* and *ROSZ* for *roses*, just like other children his age.

In the end, the focus of Cindy's research report was the enigma of Bobby and what she had learned about reading and using children to help teach reading. She did get her story told. It was a breakthrough in reading for Bobby and a triumph in writing for Cindy. She entitled the piece "Two Learners Learning."

Her district asked if they could publish her report in the local school newspaper. She agreed and added a conclusion to it suggesting that other teachers interested in learning how to write should join her that summer: she was going to run a writers' guild herself, like the one that had helped her. She wrote: "That experience taught me that it's extremely important for teachers to experience what it means to be in a supportive writing environment. Our past experience with writing is our enemy. Until we actually write together and experience what it means to support each other there's no way to help our children. Even if you now think you hate writing, join me. I promise you, you'll love the experience and be a head taller for having come."

Story 7: Students as resource

The teachers in King Elementary School consider themselves whole language teachers. Over the last two years they've introduced journal writing, the author's circle, theme studies and literature groups into their kindergarten through sixth-grade classes. For the most part they liked what they saw happening, but they often felt unsure. Did their literature discussions take the students to the depth of the literature experience? Were revisions and editing procedures taking responsibility away from the learners? What was the most effective way of responding to worried parents about the role of non-standard spelling, grammar and handwriting? What about evaluation procedures imposed from a skills model onto a whole language curriculum? Could they risk the removal of basals — and why did it feel so risky? Would their school's scores on state mandated tests drop? Were they really whole language teachers? What should they read next? What were the next steps?

The teachers talked among themselves and got good feedback from their TAWL group members, but the anxious questions didn't stop.

During this time two university teacher educators and two graduate students made a round of school visits. Their own discussions had led them to believe they needed an ongoing relationship with children and teachers in a school. In particular they were eager to observe what happened in a whole language school as children progressed from grade to grade with teachers who all shared the same model.

The two groups met at TAWL meeting and experienced that joyous and soul-satisfying human experience: convergence of enthusiasm and interests. It led to a spontaneous and two-sided invitation: "Will you folks come to King School and work with us?" "May we visit your school and your classrooms?" It really didn't take long to make the commitment, agree to conditions and create a calendar.

The first suggestions and inquiry came from the teachers. "Let's make this a research project as well as professional development. We'd like to do miscue analysis with our readers because that will tell us some specific things about them. It will also provide us with some statistics for the administration to admire. We want to share what our kids are doing. We invite you into our classrooms. We want to talk with you."

The teacher educators provided the next suggestions. "Could we meet for a few minutes before classes start, to schedule our day? And after school for discussion? How about selecting nine children from each class for miscue analysis? What will be the topic of our first after school meeting?"

For one whole school year the university folk met with the school folk on Fridays, as a group. The two graduate students came more often to get the miscue analysis done. As time progressed, research questions and procedures unfolded, and by the end of the school year everyone felt a great deal of satisfaction about professional growth and development.

"The cards" became a crucial element of the research design, one that provided a historical perspective and a trail of evidence. Every Friday morning the teachers gave their university collaborators three medium-sized (4" x 6") cards. The first, the "up-side" card, gave a brief account of one or two things that had gone well during the week:

- Jean helped Hal select a topic for his next thematic research.
- Usually silent Adrian volunteered to tell a story to the class.
- An article by Frank Smith shed light on a nagging problem.
- A parent asked questions about procedures that would promote a love of books, then volunteered to read with the children.

In contrast to this card that shared good news and invited rejoicing, the second card was the "downer." It contained notes on things that hadn't gone well, situations that had run amuck, strategies that had bombed:

- I've invited Jane again and again to participate in discussions, but obviously she isn't interested.
- There was so much racket in the room that two of the kids put their hands over their ears and Randy yelled "Shut your mouths before I shut them for you!"
- My conference with Terry's mother was a disaster. I didn't get my point across and I'm sure she thinks I didn't really listen to her.
- I read the articles you brought me last week and feel like such a dummy. Can we talk about them?

The third card was a request card:

- Let's talk about evaluation this afternoon.
- I need a list of content area trade books.
- I've listened to my miscue tape of Rosie and need to talk about her miscues and her retelling.
- What's the best way of selecting titles for our next literature study?

The cards became the basis of the after-school discussions. The talk was therefore relevant and immediately applicable. To-the-point theory was discussed as much as or more than practice. Every researcher, university or children's teacher, had a voice, a piece of the action, a right to set agenda.

And yet there was a missing link, an anomaly: many questions could only be answered by the children. Into that dilemma stepped the principal, a contributing member of the group. She suggested that some children be asked to meet with the group. The suggestion was received enthusiastically and soon the topic for the following Friday was set and the student participants selected. The principal contacted the parents, who were delighted that their children were held in such high regard.

From that day, "students as resource" became part of the after school meetings. A kindergarten child solved a problem about the lack of lively discussion following the introduction of a new big book: in a devastating observation about the quality of the book he said shyly, "There ain't nothin' there to talk about." A fifth-grader caused everyone to gasp when he solved the problem of whether or not a particular book that had been loved in the fourth grade should be included again in the fifth grade collection: "Just think of my reading it last year as my rough draft." The children's discussion about the difference between basal reader ability grouping and literature study interest grouping set the adults on their pedagogical heels. Nine-year-olds talked about the shame of being in the low group, of the helplessness of trying to get out from under a label: "You get in a group in first grade and you're there for life. Forget it."

On one level the year at King Elementary School ended as it began: students and teachers entered their classrooms every day full of enthusiasm and ready for new challenges. But on another level it ended very differently: teachers and students had begun to think about themselves as inquirers, as researchers. More, they saw themselves as collaborators — with one another and with those other learners from the university.

Story 8: Expert projects

"If you want to begin a process reading and writing curriculum in your classroom I strongly recommend you begin by creating a classroom library," said Cynthia at a local inservice meeting of special education teachers.

How, you might ask, does someone ever get confident enough to make statements of this sort? If you knew Cynthia you'd be even more surprised.

Cynthia had been a competent and confident special education teacher for 15 years. For most of that time she'd been a Skinnerian, believing in Assertive Discipline, Behavior Management and Mastery Learning. Every one of her students had an IEP — Individualized Experience Plan — and every objective of her teaching was specified in advance. Yet here she was recommending something as loosey-goosey as process reading and writing.

Cynthia's story began when Diane, a former teacher at the Rochester Developmental Learning Center, decided to go for an advanced degree. As she discovered what children already know about reading and writing before they come to school, she became convinced that the approaches being used in special education were misguided. She made up her mind to do something about it: set up a demonstration classroom, a place where other special educators could go and see for themselves what their alternatives were when it came to teaching reading and writing.

Her professors gave her the names of several special education teachers in the local area. Diane wanted a teacher who was concerned and dedicated and who believed in what she was doing, but not necessarily a like-minded colleague.

Cynthia fit the bill. She was interested in integrating reading and writing in her program, and together Diane and Cynthia decided to select this as a mutual topic of interest. Each day they met to discuss planned activities. Afterwards they explored how they might further integrate reading and writing in any one activity, with concrete suggestions for specific lessons. It was only later that they began to rethink the whole curriculum, especially standard curriculum approaches for special learners.

Early in their relationship Diane's prompting led them to the decision to both teach and research, to both "do" and "reflect." They each planned lessons and jointly explored ways to integrate reading and writing. They reflected on how they could make their lessons theoretically consistent with what the profession was discovering about language learning.

The creation of a classroom library was one project they undertook. Cynthia initially wanted everything very structured. After all, she'd spent the first half of the year getting the children to stay in their seats, and Diane's ideas for a classroom library looked like a free-for-all to her. There was no way she was going to let the discipline she'd fought for go out the window. But Diane argued that the children needed to be involved from the beginning. After a good deal of discussion and thinking they decided to have the students plan the project.

As a first step Diane and Cynthia pointed out that the children were requesting more and more books and that they often had to wait for their choices to be available. How about building a classroom library? Getting an enthusiastic response, they asked what the students thought was needed to create one.

Recommendations ranged from what materials would be needed to build the library (cinder blocks and boards) to where such materials might be obtained. Once they had decided on a location, the next question was how to figure out what books to include and where to get them. The children decided to do a survey of classroom interests and bring books in from home, as well as ask the school librarian for suggestions.

They divided themselves into work groups and over the next couple of days met to carry out their goals. One child's parents donated the lumber, another the cinder blocks, a third the paint. This group of three built the library while the others conducted interest surveys and tabulated results. A small group took the results to the librarian and got permission to keep 100 books in their class library for a month, after which the collection would be changed.

It wasn't long, once the library was complete, before Danny asked for a class meeting. He felt there wasn't enough time in the school day to use the library.

Others suggested that they do projects involving the books. These became known as "expert projects." During a classroom session the students each picked a topic and wrote down on small (3" x 5") pieces of paper everything they already knew about it — one item per slip. In the next session they wrote down the things they wanted to learn. In a third session they listed resources that could help them find the information they needed, both books and community resources.

Danny was interested in lizards. He decided to interview a naturalist at a local state park. Jules was interested in horses. He decided to interview a local farmer and a high school student who rode horses competitively.

All students were invited to do the best they could in collecting their information, and to write whatever they found on the slips of paper. Diane and Cynthia assured them they needn't to be able to read everything in a book. Their advice was:

- Start with the pictures and captions, then look for other text you can read.
- Ask one of the teachers or another student to help you read the stuff you think may be important.
- Feel free to take books home and have your parents read sections to you.
- Don't worry about spelling, use "kid's writing." "Adult writing" will be used later, for the final publication of projects.

A portion of each day was set aside for expert projects. Saddi brought in a snail and asked, "Would a snail fall off the edge of a table or would it turn around before it crashed to the floor?" Everyone, including Cynthia and Diane, held their breath as Saddi set up her experiment and tabulated the results. Fortunately the snail had enough sense to turn around each and every time it came to the edge of a table. It even maneuvered up the edge of a pencil, over the eraser and down the other side!

Once the students had collected a fair amount of information on their topics the teachers provided support for sorting it out and putting it in report form. The children were encouraged to read through their slips of paper and group them into categories, then think about pictures that could illustrate some of the information. They could draw these or find them in other books — sometimes good artists were "contracted" by other authors to draw particularly difficult illustrations. Once they had pictures, the students were invited to transcribe from the slips whatever information they saw as relevant. In this manner each child produced a lengthy report, a first for most of them. They shared their reports eagerly, and most already had a topic for their next expert project by the time they were done.

Cynthia and Diane learned a great deal. Both began to question the notion that children not doing well in school need more basics, more skills and drills. All children, not just average or "bright" ones, need opportunities to use reading and writing for learning. These children had rarely experienced what it means to be a reader, but now they began to see themselves not only as readers but as authors. With this perception in place, the progress they made in reading and writing over the course of the year was incredible.

Second, these two teachers learned how important it is for students to take ownership of the classroom. They already understood the importance of making children owners of reading and writing, but they had never explored the importance of this concept for the classroom itself. The classroom library project taught the children to think of the classroom as theirs as well as the teacher's. They continued to recommend all sorts of changes. By the end of the year they all had personal bulletin board space where they could post things of importance to them, a work area where they could do their projects, and a "quiet" area where they could go to "just do nothing, like read."

You can imagine that Cynthia's presentation to her fellow special education teachers not only started but also ended strong. She closed the session on this note: "In June the principal visited my room. He stayed the whole morning. When he left he said something very important. 'You know, Cynthia, these kids don't look like special education kids to me.' I couldn't resist it. I said, 'That may not be the children's problem but your problem, what you think about special education children.'"

Story 9: Writing a book

We did manage to write this book in the short time we had together, as planned. We stayed in a comfortable house, ate too much delicious food, and talked and fought and typed and revised and laughed and argued — and ate some more.

Even we find it difficult to tell who is specifically responsible for which parts. It truly represents a collaborative effort. Let us share with you what we learned.

Jerry

As I drove to where we would write this book I kept asking myself this: How will Watson and Burke get their wish into this book that "curriculum" and "inquiry" be synonyms? They did. And in the process I relearned why it is we can trust the learning process. I rediscovered what it means to collaborate rather than cooperate: when we cooperate we work towards some mutual goal, but when we collaborate we expect to go out changed in the end, to become a different person. I've come to understand why I feel so strongly that reflexivity and humility are vitally important: they keep me learning and guard my self-respect. I've learned why it is we all need editors, and how face-to-face interaction is key to the creation of a thought collective.

Carol

Panic stations! Yes, I want to help write this book. But I'm claustrophobic at the thought of being trapped with others looking over my shoulder while I — the slowest writer in the West — attempt to organize my thoughts on paper. Will I be able to compose under these time constraints and in this close physical environment? I know that my hang-up with writing is a leftover from the old models of learning that shaped my early schooling. Fortunately miscue research rescued me from many of my early concerns about the nature of research, language instruction and convention. But I still agonize and agonize over writing.

This experience has provided me with a strengthened regard for the powers of collaboration and an awareness of the impact of improved language tools (the computer), but more than that, with a new appreciation of the ultimate power of continued engagement. Never again will I be forced to work in isolation!

Dorothy

A book in four days? Ridiculous! Writing takes time.

When I thought of my usual approach — beg grad students and other friends to read every paragraph, talk to me for hours and make lots of suggestions — I was faced with a humbling realization: I don't write without a great deal of support and encouragement. But then, who better than Carol and Jerry to provide it? No question that we share the same beliefs about literacy and whole language curriculum. It's also true that they believe in and trust collaborative efforts. And, thank goodness, they both take a lot of food breaks and have a sense of humor. We could give it a try.

Questions about organization and structure were up front, but the major focus of inquiry, at least the one that directed me, was this: how could we accurately capture what we've learned from whole language teachers, kids and parents. Then, having used their wisdom and experiences, how could we repay their generosity in our writing?

This book confirms the strength of a collaborative effort. I sometimes got off the mark, took wrong turns, became discouraged. But there was always someone to get me started again, to renew my spirit. When I sat staring into that pale green screen, brain dead, someone would nudge me into the "discomfort zone of my proximal development." I learned as much from those stumbling times as I did from the periods when my writing flowed easily. I learned because of Jerry and Carolyn, because of our editor-teacher-learner Adrian, and because of all the images of teachers and kids held in the back of my head.

Invitation: Your story

- "Plan to plan" your wish.
- Live your wish.
- Write your story: "My Wish."

An open letter to learners

Dear Colleague:

In 1986 Ken Goodman wrote his Bright Idea book *What's Whole in Whole Language*. We see our book as its companion. In it we've tried to point out the direction we hope the whole language movement will take.

As Ken explains in his book, whole language is a theory of language and a theory of learning. In tandem, these theories have revolutionized the profession's thinking about language learning and how it can best be supported in classrooms. Teachers like you have found whole language a heady experience for children, as well as for yourselves. It's made this an exciting time to be in education.

What you may not have realized yet is that whole language is also a theory of professional development — and it's this component that keeps the others full of vim and vigor. It ensures that, as a theory of language and of learning, whole language will never stagnate and turn into just another educational orthodoxy. It provides a built-in self-correction device, for the theory itself and for the profession as a whole.

At one level, this book simply captures a number of items we personally have come to realize create a sense of urgency within us. It's our curriculum wish book. It doesn't contain curricular recipes, but issues invitations to a future that can be realized only in collaboration. And here is our stake in it, ours and yours: we transform education into inquiry and learning into a universal curriculum.

In the past, teaching has been seen as distinct from inquiry. Research was something college professors did, teaching something school teachers knew about. Colleges and universities were engaged in knowledge production, teachers and schools in knowledge distribution and use. This separation of theory and practice created a two-tiered system. Researchers and theorizers reigned above teachers. Researchers' voices were given priority, teachers' voices were silenced.

Now we know better. For a number of years already we've been hearing comments like the following from the mouths of speakers at teachers' conventions: "There's nothing more practical than theory, and nothing as theoretical as practice." This book is an effort to take this phrase beyond its superficial appeal. What propels us to professional growth are the constant moves within us between theory and practice. When these moves encounter blockage — anomalies — we inquire why and begin the process of creating new meanings.

From the perspective of whole language, teaching as inquiry is the theory of "voice." Just as democracies are enriched by hearing all voices, so whole language and the profession of teaching will be enriched by your inquiring voice, and those of others. There's no need to apologize for where you are in the whole language scheme of things. There are no prior qualifications for accepting our invitations except that you bring an inquiring mind willing to be used. No question will be too small, no concern too trivial. Nor do you need to back off because you've come to see yourself as "humanist," "intuitive" or "artsy." Some (perhaps all) of the best thinkers in education have been just that.

You may, in fact, want to begin by doing one of the many things you have a hunch will improve your language arts program. Commit yourself to one of your wishes — and to a second as well: to get it done. Invite a colleague to help you, a faculty member at a local university, a fellow teacher, one or more of your students, the principal, a curriculum coordinator. Begin by "planning to plan," thinking about what things have stopped you from doing what you know to be professionally sound. Undertake to systematically remove these restraints. No teacher should be stopped from implementing what he or she truly believes is the best curriculum possible. Learners grow by reaching for the ideal.

Often, professional development activities set up by schools and districts cater to weak teachers rather than to strong ones. Whole language teachers constantly complain to us that they've had to sit through yet one more insipid program. What's being presented is often a step backwards from what strong teachers already know, especially about language, learning and the curriculum. Such practices must stop. Education can grow only when it builds up from its strongest resources, not from its weakest ones.

All this relates to the issue of trust. Within the old model of research, each participant weighs all the others on an adversarial scale. The hierarchical model prevails; the research clan knows who the lightweights and heavyweights are. Not trust, but competition fuels the research.

Classroom teachers don't even make it to the scales. They are considered irrelevant to the "production of knowledge." Knowledge is assembled and stored with the researchers and then packaged for teachers in textbooks. Teachers aren't trusted to know anything. Teacher-bashing has become a national pastime.

This isn't just a North American phenomenon. In April 1987, the Dutch media broadcast the news that third-year education students had not scored well on a math test drawn from sixth-grade math texts. "How can we let them loose on classrooms?" was the media's cry. The usual letters to the editor and comments by media gurus bemoaned and bemoaned. The air was filled with a giant absence of trust in education students and practicing teachers.

Ironically, these future teachers were already using a good deal of math in the ordinary course of their daily lives. They were expected to make and live by personal budgets, to buy wisely and complete their income tax returns — to name just a few math practicalities they'd deal with daily. And as far as teaching was concerned, these education students would work hard to make sure that what had to be taught they could teach.

Mistrust of teachers is showing itself also in the ever expanding and more detailed teaching guides that accompany text series. Publishers assure textbook adoption committees that their stuff is "teacher proof," meaning that no matter how stupid teachers may be, the program will still succeed.

The professional development side of whole language looks at the very existence of text series — especially basal reading series, their teaching guides and accompanying paraphernalia — as prima facie evidence of the prevailing mistrust of classroom teachers. So who should be surprised that current professional development presents teachers over and over again with the same meagre diet of insipid information? And has teachers sit, and sit, and sit some more?

We reiterate our invitation for you to take control of your own professional destiny, to trust yourself. And demand to be trusted by others. The result will be that you'll come to trust your students.

There's yet one more crucial issue implicit in all we've said. We love errors and invite you to love them too. Nothing should scare you more than groups or persons who think they know all the answers. Good learners always encounter errors that make them itch professionally.

On the theoretical level, "error" means that at least one of the tenets of a particular theory doesn't wash, and we've talked about this as a thrust towards inquiry. In fact, we'd say that good inquirers know an important reality: that wallowing in correctness, being hell-bent for "mastery," stops learning. Messes are the fodder of creativity. Thinking through what is initially seen as an error makes new insights possible. The longer you involve yourself in inquiry, the more you'll cherish messes. They'll become signs that you're about to grow. Under the best conditions, anomalies force you to develop a new perspective on the world.

Miscue analysis, the resolution of an error, turned into what is now called "the whole language movement." Old models of reading didn't adequately explain what the readers in Ken Goodman's study were doing. Miscue analysis provided a new hypothesis about how the reading process worked. It revolutionized the way the profession thought about reading and reading instruction.

Research in early literacy created another major shift. Using children as informants, researchers found that the beliefs about how children learn language were wrong. Observations of young children's actual reading and writing didn't support previous beliefs that there's an inherent order in language itself that dictates how language needs to be learned (the skills model of language learning), or that there's an inherent order in the way learners learn language (the developmental model).

The question was, what might an alternative explanation be? One hypothesis now being tested is the more powerful construct for understanding both knowledge and learning: experience. Children who have a lot of experience with print seem to know more about it than those who haven't, despite age or cognitive development. If we see experience as sets of demonstrations, and define demonstrations operationally as the things people in the learner's community do as they use language in the ordinary courses of their lives, then we've planted the seeds for a social theory of language learning, and of learning as inquiry.

Error isn't a faulty by-product of inquiry, it's inquiry's lifeblood and driving force. Fortunately we seem to live in a world akin to a first draft, and there's lots of inquiring for all of us to do. Error is not only guaranteed, it's an international human resource. Would that learners valued error more. Even many whole language teachers have only just begun to tolerate it. When learners value error, they operate much differently.

For instance, teachers who value error teach reading differently. Instead of having students read a selection and then retell it, they help them focus on what didn't make sense. They help students interrogate the text, as well as any assumptions they brought to help set up a framework of predictions for the reading task.

Fortunately the human mind has a natural penchant for focusing on the new and anomalous. The trick for becoming an inquirer is to harness this penchant for the sake of learning. That's what this book has tried to demonstrate, and what we believe whole language must cultivate in the years to come.

Happy inquiry from us all.

Dorothy Watson   *Carolyn Burke*

Jerome Harste

The *Bright Idea* Series

In *Bright Idea* books, gifted authors reveal to readers the hearts of their professional lives. What has excited them professionally? What have they spent their years discovering, and why?

In these books they dress some old truths in new styles, and reveal some new truths about children, about language, about learning, about teachers, teaching and parenting.

The series was conceived and is published in Canada, but the authors come from all over: the United States, New Zealand, The Netherlands, Great Britain, Canada.

So far twelve titles have been published:

☞	**The Craft of Children's Writing**	Judith Newman
	Grand Conversations: **Literature Groups in Action**	Ralph Peterson and Maryann Eeds
	Learning Computer Learning	Veronica Buckley and Martin Lamb
	Other Countries, Other Schools	Mike Bruce
☞	**Reading Begins at Birth**	David B. Doake
☞	**Spel . . . Is a Four-Letter Word**	J. Richard Gentry
	Tests: Marked for Life?	S. Alan Cohen
	The Tone of Teaching	Max van Manen
☞	**What's Whole in Whole Language?**	Ken Goodman
	When School Is a Struggle	Curt Dudley-Marling
☞	**Whole Language: Inquiring Voices**	Dorothy Watson, Carolyn Burke and Jerome Harste
	A Word is a Word . . . Or Is It?	Michael Graves

In Canada, order from Scholastic Canada Ltd., 123 Newkirk Road, Richmond Hill, Ontario L4C 3G5.

In the United States, order from Scholastic Inc., P.O. Box 7502, Jefferson City, MO 65102.

☞ Available in New Zealand and Australia through Ashton Scholastic, and in the United Kingdom through Scholastic Publications.